The Good Dog Library

Canine Medicine

Common Conditions, Diseases & Treatments

ISBN: 0-9758716-3-3

Tufts Media Enterprises
200 Boston Ave., Suite 3500
Medford, MA 02155 USA

Cover photo: Andrew Cunningham, TUSVM

Canine Medicine
Common Conditions, Diseases & Treatments
The editors of *Your Dog*

ISBN: 0-9758716-3-3
1. Canine-Medicine   2. Dogs-Care   3. Dogs-Medical
4. Canine-Veterinary

Manufactured in the United States of America

The Good Dog Library

Canine Medicine

Common Conditions, Diseases & Treatments

Scientific Editor: Armelle de Laforcade

Assistant Professor
Tufts Cummings School of Veterinary Medicine
North Grafton, MA

Contents

Section II: Conditions

Section III: Bones & Joints

Section IV: Prevention, Treatment & First Aid

Introduction

When it comes to our health these days, the emphasis is on wellness. Eat right, keep your weight down, and establish a regular exercise regimen, and you'll be in a lot better shape to battle the health challenges that come your way. The same could be said for your dog.

Your dog depends on you to help protect his or her health. That means limiting treats and kibble, providing mental stimulation and love, keeping your pet physically active, and, most importantly, establishing a relationship with your veterinarian.

Canine Medicine: Common Conditions, Diseases & Treatments provides information about the causes and treatments for some of today's most troubling dog health problems. In Section I: Diseases and Disorders, you'll learn about canine cancer, which strikes more than half of today's older dogs. We also have information about ailments to which senior dogs are particularly vulnerable, such as canine cognitive dysfunction syndrome. And, on the positive side, we share exciting information about new techniques for helping dogs with heart problems.

Section II focuses on conditions such as eye, ear, skin, and respiratory problems. We'll provide insights about symptoms for which you need to watch out and explain treatments your veterinarian may recommend.

Section III is all about bones and joints. This is where you'll find information about arthritis, dysplasia, and intervertebral disk disease. Yes, dogs too can have and benefit from hip replacement and back surgeries.

Finally, in Section IV, we look at prevention, treatment, and first aid. You'll learn how to perform canine CPR and the Heimlich maneuver in case of emergency. There's information on how to head off serious problems with parasites. We'll explain why we are strong advocates for neutering or spaying your dog. And, we'll share tips on finding clinical trials that may be coming up for your dog's ailment and on how to make the most of your visit to the veterinarian.

That last point—maximizing your time with the veterinarian through keeping notes on changes in your dog's behavior—cannot be overemphasized. While this book is full of valuable information, no book or Web site can substitute for regular visits to your veterinarian. Let this be your guide as you read this book. If your dog is limping, panting excessively, eating more or less than usual, or is exhibiting other signs of change or distress, stop reading and go to the vet. Your dog will thank you for it. ■

Armelle de Laforcade
Assistant Professor
Tufts University School of Veterinary Medicine
DVM, Diplomate of the American College of Veterinary Emergency
and Critical Care

Section I

Diseases & Disorders

1

Canine Cancer

With early detection and improved treatment, canine cancer doesn't have to be a death sentence.

They are among the words you least want to hear: your dog has cancer. But the odds are that you will hear them someday. One in four dogs get cancer; half of the dogs over ten years old die from or with some form of cancer. Still, such a diagnosis isn't always a reason for total despair. Refined treatments, an increasing number of options, and groundbreaking research are saving lives.

"Cancer isn't necessarily a death sentence," says Dr. John Berg, veterinary surgeon and chair of the Department of Clinical Sciences at Tufts University School of Veterinary Medicine. "In most cases, there is something good we can do."

Indeed, Dr. Philip Bergman, head of the Donaldson-Atwood Cancer Clinic at the Animal Medical Center in New York City and president of the Veterinary Cancer Society, estimates that about half the dogs his center sees are considered cured after cancer treatment.

Much of what is known about canine cancer closely parallels what is known about cancer in humans. Dogs are at risk for the same types of cancer that afflict humans, and treating canine cancer successfully is dependent upon the same variables found in human cancer treatment: the type of cancer, the wisdom of the attending doctor in choosing the most effective course of treatment, the availability of advanced medical techniques, and the willingness and ability to pay for treatment.

There are other similarities:

- Statistically speaking, cancer is a disease of middle and old age.
- Certain cancers are largely preventable with prudent lifestyle choices.
- Early detection is almost always a critical factor.
- Cancer can be hereditary, sometimes running in canine families.
- Variables like nutrition and toxic exposure seem to play a prominent role.

Don't discount individual response to disease. For some dogs, the immune system rallies and the treatments seem magically precise. For others, treatment becomes a holding pattern, an evolving equation of modulated therapy versus quality of life. For still others, hope fades quickly.

Early Detection

Just as with humans, early detection offers the best hope for your dog's survival, particularly for those cancers that aggressively metastasize (spread to distant sites). Make it a regular practice to examine your dog's body for unexplained swelling or lumps.

However, many early warning signs of cancer are more subtle. While many of these signs—behavioral changes, loss of appetite, increased water consumption, persistent wheezing or coughing—require only basic observational skills on the part of the owner, other signs require a more sophisticated knowledge of your pet. Also, cancers are often traced to the site of earlier injuries, traumas, wounds, or fractures, so knowledge and examination of these injury sites can be helpful.

If you are buying a dog from a breeder, ask about the prevalence of cancer in that breed and in that particular canine family. Heredity is a major determining factor in cancer; it is thought that boxers, for example, are more prone to cancer than any other breed. These statistics should not necessarily make you shy away from that breed, but increase your level of vigilance.

As dogs age, they are increasingly prone to both growths on the skin and to fatty deposits just under it. Most often these growths are benign, but even a veterinarian can't reliably tell just by looking. It is crucial to aspirate (withdraw cells via a thin needle) and, if necessary, biopsy (analyze the tissue sample under a microscope) these growths upon detection.

Even benign growths should be monitored closely as they have the potential to become cancerous. In addition, a dog might have a number of seemingly identical growths, of which only one is malignant.

As your dog ages, the likelihood increases that he or she will get cancer in some form. Simple awareness can go a long way toward providing a happy outcome.

Diagnosis

If cancer is suspected, your veterinarian will order a series of tests that may include aspiration, biopsy, blood tests, urine tests, X-rays, and ultrasound.

In some cases, your veterinarian might recommend exploratory surgery or one of the advanced, accurate, and expensive scanning technologies available to human patients.

When a cancer is present, no matter how your veterinarian has arrived at the diagnosis, he or she should present you with a realistic prognosis. This process, called staging, identifies both the extent of the cancer's spread (metastasis), and determines the treatment options available.

Be Aware of Common Cancer Signs

Dogs with cancer don't show symptoms early in the disease. This means owners must watch for any changes in their pet. They should take dogs for wellness checkups twice a year, the Morris Animal Foundation advises. These checks should include a thorough hands-on examination for lumps and bumps. They're also an opportunity to discuss any observations about physical or behavioral changes in the dog.

With older or cancer-prone breeds, owners should keep an eye out for changes in energy level, appetite, stamina and behavior, including panting and coughing. These changes, which owners often believe accompany aging, aren't normal. Cancer may not be the cause, but the earlier any disease is caught, the better the chance that the dog can be treated successfully.

Cancer-prone breeds include Golden Retrievers, Rottweilers, Irish Wolfhounds, Mastiffs, German Shepherds, Labrador Retrievers, and nearly all other large and giant breeds.

Treatments

Treatment decisions involve a complex and emotional set of options, which may be limited by where you live, the range of veterinary resources available, the age of the dog, and the money you are willing or able to spend.

Surgery

When it comes to canine cancer, a tumor that can be cleanly excised is the best possible news. For certain malignant tumors, caught early, surgery provides what is still the best hope for a lasting cure. It can be combined with radiation and/or chemotherapy.

Surgery is most frequently used for mammary, lung, bone, and gastrointestinal tumors. While surgery generally is highly effective, there are the common risks—blood loss, pneumonia, infection, and so on—associated with such procedures. The dog's age and health also are factors in how well the animal will recover from surgery.

Radiation Therapy

Radiation therapy uses a series of directed bursts of radiation, more powerful than X-rays, to neutralize the cancer cells. This treatment can be highly effective in controlling localized tumors. It is also used as an adjunct to surgery in which tumors evade total removal, and

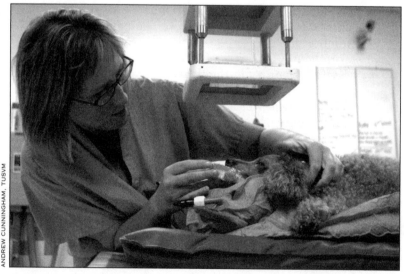

ANDREW CUNNINGHAM, TUSVM

A Miniature Poodle undergoes radiation therapy for nasal cavity cancer.

is sometimes prescribed prior to other treatments to reduce a tumor's size. Radiation therapy is a valuable, if limited, tool, given its long-term risks and side effects. It destroys normal cells in addition to the cancerous cells, so the ability of surrounding tissue to heal may be seriously impacted. In addition, radiation therapy requires a major time and monetary commitment. A typical program entails twelve treatments over four weeks.

> ❝ RADIATION IS ESPECIALLY EFFECTIVE AGAINST SMALL TUMORS LOCATED ON OR NEAR THE BODY SURFACE. ❞

Other forms of radiation, which will be discussed later in this section, have also proven helpful in treating certain localized canine cancers. "Radiation therapy often helps with tumors we can't treat with surgery or chemotherapy," says Dr. Tony Moore, a veterinary oncologist and co-founder of Veterinary Oncology Consultants (**www.vetoncologyconsults.com**) in Australia. And, recent advances in radiation therapy have enabled veterinarians to treat a greater number of tumors with fewer side effects.

Cells undergoing division (mitosis) are most susceptible to radiation's effects, but at any given time, only a small percentage of tumor cells are dividing. So to assure that radiation hits as many dividing cells as possible and to allow the normal surrounding tissue time to repair, oncologists typically give radiation in multiple doses (fractions) over several weeks. "Usually, a complete course of therapy consists of daily or every-other-day treatments over a four- to six-week period," says Dr. Moore.

Radiation kills the dividing cancer cells by damaging their twisted strands of DNA (deoxyribonucleic acid)—the material that helps the cells manufacture essential proteins. Prior to treatment, veterinarians use imaging techniques such as CT (computed tomography) scans to pinpoint the area to be irradiated. The radiation beam must be focused precisely on the tumorous target, so canine patients are anesthetized for the procedure.

Veterinary oncologists often prescribe radiation therapy before surgery to shrink tumors to an operable size or after surgery to kill residual cancer cells. Radiation is especially effective against small tumors located on or near the body surface, such as mast cell tumors. Radiation therapy is also useful for treating oral, nasal, and some types of brain tumors if they are located in areas where surgical removal is difficult or risky. However, radiation therapy is not effective against systemic cancers such as leukemia or metastatic tumors that have spread from their original site.

The recent availability (albeit limited) of high-energy megavoltage radiation for veterinary patients has given a boost to cancer treatment. Although orthovoltage radiation is commonly available in veterinary practice, this lower-energy radiation starts depositing its energy as soon as it hits the skin surface and is thus practical only for superficial tumors. "And to get an effective dose to the tumor, you may have to expose the skin to a large amount of radiation," says Dr. Moore. The skin burns typically caused by orthovoltage radiation are itchy and painful for the dog until they heal.

Megavoltage radiation circumvents some of the drawbacks of orthovoltage therapy. When veterinarians deliver it through a linear accelerator, megavoltage radiation can treat deeply seated tumors—and with great precision. "With a linear accelerator, we can treat a chest-wall tumor without damaging the underlying lung tissue," says Dr. Moore. Megavoltage radiation is also less damaging to your dog's skin because most of the radiational energy is released beneath the skin.

Tufts and many other veterinary schools as well as some private referral practices, offer megavoltage radiation treatments.

Chemotherapy

In general, chemotherapy (treatment with drugs) has not yet lived up to its early promise. This is because, in the simplest terms, it is an unfocused strategy that attacks all fast-growing cells, including those of the immune system. Also, as a tumor grows and spreads, there exists a high probability of concomitant cell growth resistant to whatever chemotherapy is applied to it.

Nevertheless, chemotherapy remains a mainstay of cancer treatment, and can offer hope to owners of many dogs with various kinds of cancer. There is an enormous amount of research under way, particularly in the field of immuno-targeted drugs, designed to specifically seek out only cancerous cells, reducing or eliminating chemo's signature compromise of a patient's immune system. Some ultimately fatal cancers, like lymphosarcoma, respond particularly well to current chemotherapy protocols, often adding many worthwhile months to a dog's life.

New treatment techniques are emerging, amputation is still the therapy of choice for dogs with osteosarcoma since it removes both the primary cancer site and the primary source of pain.

These days, veterinarians often use a combination of drugs that target only cancer cells and have fewer side effects. In addition, dogs tend to handle the lower doses of chemotherapy better than humans. They usually don't experience hair loss and nausea. In fact, some owners report their dogs seem immediately improved because the therapy eases tumors' effects on the body.

"Nobody should make a decision about radiation or chemotherapy due to a preconceived notion," Dr. Berg says. "Get the facts from your veterinarian or specialist."

Other Therapies

■ **Photodynamic Therapy:** In photodynamic therapy, or PDT, the patient is injected with a light-sensitive agent that precisely marks the tumor. It is then possible to apply a laser with minimal damage to surrounding tissue. Among the advantages over radiation, it is often a one-time treatment, less expensive, less intrusive for the patient, and less time-consuming for the pet owner. Photodynamic therapy is not widely available.

■ **Bone Therapy:** Osteosarcoma accounts for some 80 percent of the primary bone tumors found in dogs. Some researchers are exploring a technique called bone transport that might eventually eliminate amputation as the treatment of choice in some early-stage bone cancer patients.

In this procedure, after the surgical removal of the cancerous part of the limb, a cross-sectional piece of the patient's normal bone is moved into place, held by what is called an Ilizarov brace. Because it is the patient's own bone, with a blood supply in place, the body responds as it would to a fracture. The brace is moved as the bone heals naturally behind it; when the new bone structure is complete, the brace is removed.

It should be emphasized that, while promising, this technique remains experimental.

■ **Immunotherapy:** This treatment is familiar to anyone who's ever had an allergy shot. Basically, it manipulates, or "tricks," the immune system into protecting against specific infectious agents. There is a great deal of research under way in this field, and reason to hope that in the not-too-distant future, veterinarians will be able to regulate dogs' immune system to attack the specific characteristics of specific cancers. One area of this research involves genetically engineered vaccines for melanoma and several other types of cancer. Cancer begins when the immune system is unable to identify or destroy cancerous cells. Vaccines might effectively utilize the fact that melanoma, for example, carries unique antigens (shorthand for antibody-generating) on the surface of its cells. As of this writing, cancer vaccines are available only through clinical trials.

■ **Marrow transplants:** Tufts and the University of Massachusetts Memorial Health Care Center's Cancer Center collaborated on a study to improve remission duration in both humans and dogs with lymphoma. The study investigated how autologous bone marrow transplants (marrow cells removed from and subsequently returned to the same patient) might enable canine lymphoma patients to safely receive higher-than-usual doses of chemotherapy.

Bone marrow transplantation for lymphoma patients is not new. However, existing techniques used megadoses of chemotherapy drugs that not only kill cancer cells but also obliterate the neutrophils and lymphocytes manufactured in the patient's bone marrow. Because these white blood cells contribute to your dog's immune system, a dearth of healthy marrow leaves a dog vulnerable to infection.

Five lymphoma-afflicted dogs owned by Tufts clients went through this complex procedure:

■ First, veterinarians biospied the patient's bone marrow to make sure lymphoma cells had not yet infiltrated those tissues.

■ Then the patients received a nine-week course of standard chemotherapy to push the disease into remission.

■ Next, the patients received a growth factor to "rev up" the bone marrow before harvesting for future implantation. To do that, veterinarians used a hypodermic needle inserted in the anesthetized dog's upper foreleg bone to withdraw marrow. The marrow was then mixed with a nutrient medium, filtered to remove blood clots, then frozen at an extremely low temperature.

■ Finally, after a two-week break to allow the patient to recover from the preparatory procedures, veterinarians administered a higher than usual dose of the chemotherapy drug cyclophosphamide.

"We worked our way up gradually and found the highest effective dosage that wouldn't cause excessive negative side effects," says Dr. Angela Frimberger, a veterinary oncologist who was involved in the study while at Tufts. She is now director and co-founder of Veterinary Oncology Consultants (**www.vetoncologyconsults.com**) in Australia. "Although the treatment was a little more time-consuming for dog owners and veterinarians, toxicity was not worsened by the increased dose intensity of chemotherapy, and that was the first of our two primary goals. The second goal was to see if the increased dose intensity, while not more toxic, would be more effective. The dogs in the study that were treated at the highest dose had remission times more than twice as long on average than the dogs treated in the lower dose groups or with standard-dose chemotherapy. The cure rate for these dogs will probably also be about twice that for dogs treated with traditional chemotherapy."

Dr. Frimberger adds: "This treatment is somewhat more expensive and more complicated than traditional therapy for dogs with lymphoma and it isn't for everybody, but for selected dogs it has the potential to provide a significant advantage against their cancer."

Lymphoma

Lymphoma is a cancer of the blood cells and tissues associated with the lymphatic system. Generally afflicting middle-aged and older dogs, it is a cancer whose most common type involves multiple external lymph nodes. Other forms originate in the gastrointestinal tract, chest, skin, or bone marrow.

Frequently examine your dog's body for abnormalities; it is of particular importance here, as lymphoma is one of the most common cancers diagnosed in dogs. It is usually a simple matter to locate swollen lymph nodes at the base of the jaws, in the rear legs behind the knee, armpits, groin, and in front of the shoulder blades.

While true cures, for all practical purposes, remain out of reach, lymphoma responds exceptionally well to chemotherapy. And, innovative bone marrow transplant studies have raised hope for improved chemotherapy protocols and longer remission times. What constitutes an acceptable quality of life, however, will sooner or later be the overriding issue for you as a dog owner.

Dr. Lisa Barber, a Tufts clinical assistant professor and veterinary oncologist, is working with other oncologists nationally to standardize definitions and descriptions of clinical signs of canine lymphoma. The goal is to improve the ability to determine whether certain signs have significance in determining the cancer's prognosis.

Be Wary of Holistic Treatments

Some pet owners turn to holistic or alternative medicine when they learn their dog has cancer. Before you decide to try holistic medicine, talk to the veterinarian or veterinary oncologist.

Many cancers and tumors are treatable and have a good prognosis in early stages using conventional methods.

Holistic methods may appear to work, but aren't approved by the U.S. Food and Drug Administration. Nor is there adequate research to prove they cure any cancers.

Many veterinarians are open to trying alternative methods, provided that they don't interfere with the conventional treatment.

Before you consider trying an herb supplement, homeopathic medicine, or other alternative therapy, talk to the veterinarian to make sure it won't cause problems with your dog's current treatment.

Osteosarcoma

This aggressively malignant bone cancer most often strikes large or giant breeds, typically in the long bones of the legs. It almost always spreads, or metastasizes, to distant sites before it is diagnosed. Osteosarcoma tends to spread to the lungs very early in the course of the disease, and accounts for some 80 percent of the primary bone cancers found in dogs. The median age at diagnosis is seven years. However, osteosarcoma has been seen in small dogs and those as young as six months.

Normal bone contains cells called osteoclasts, whose job is to break down and remove old bone cells so new cells can replace them. In osteosarcoma, bones contain too many osteoclasts. The tumor expands outward as it destroys bone cells. The bone becomes fragile, sometime riddled with microfractures and with interior bleeding. It may break with minor injury. The break, called a pathologic fracture, doesn't heal, because the bone-destroying cells crowd out bone-building cells. A pathologic fracture causes intense pain.

Veterinarians diagnose more than eight thousand canine cases a year. A presumptive diagnosis can almost always be made based on the radiographs of the limb, but biopsy is sometimes necessary. Osteosarcoma sometimes is misdiagosed as a mere sprain. Its common early symptom is lameness, which worsens over one to three months until the dog won't put weight on the leg any longer.

Treatment Options

While new treatment techniques are emerging, amputation is still the therapy of choice since it removes both the primary cancer site and the primary source of pain. With amputation alone, however, only 10 percent of patients survive one year. When chemotherapy is applied, the one-year survival increases to 50 percent. You'll find more information about chemotherapy and radiation therapy elsewhere in this chapter.

Although many owners are initially very upset by the prospect of an amputation, the procedure is actually very well tolerated by the overwhelming majority of dogs. Most dogs continue to live a very normal life after an amputation, and do not suffer negative psychological effects as a person might.

Chemotherapy usually is given after amputation. It combats any remaining cancer cells, including those that travel to the lungs and other organs. It's administered three to five times, depending on the drug, over three to four months, beginning about two weeks after surgery.

Some common chemotherapy drugs are cisplatin and doxorubicin. Cisplatin improves survival time 180 to 400 days and one-year survival rates 30 percent to 62 percent. With doxorubicin, median survival is 365 days, and 10 percent of dogs live two years after surgery.

Radiation therapy of a primary bone tumor is also a palliative treatment used primarily to reduce tumor pain. According to radiation oncologists at Tufts University School of Veterinary Medicine's Harrington Oncology Program, about 70 percent of dogs treated with radiation therapy have a significant reduction in pain and can retain use of the leg. The life expectancy for a dog receiving palliative radiation alone is about four to six months.

Radiation can be re-administered when pain returns. Veterinarians caution that about one-third of dogs don't respond to radiation and, among those whose pain is relieved, the possibility of fracture increases because the dog feels better and is more active.

Pain-relief medicines, such as carprofen, etodolac and aspirin, may provide some relief in early stages of osteosarcoma, but they're unable to fight overwhelming pain later.

In combination with chemotherapy, limb-sparing surgery may be an option for dogs who are not good candidates for amputation. These include very heavy dogs and those with orthopedic or neurological problems. Bone transport, described above, is one experimental technique for limb-sparing surgery. In another technique, the primary bone tumor is removed and a donated bone (allograft) is grafted in its place. A polymer implant containing the chemotherapeutic drug cisplatin may be wrapped around the allograft to reduce the risk of local recurrence of the tumor.

Because the bone graft must be "fixed" in place, the adjacent joint also becomes fixed. For this reason, limb salvage is only effective for tumors of the distal radius, or wrist. The limb-sparing procedure carries the risk of allograft rejection and infection. Because of the complexity of the procedure, limb-sparing surgery is performed at a limited number of veterinary referral clinics and teaching hospitals. A successful procedure results in a leg that is both functional and cosmetically appealing. Survival times with limb-sparing surgery are similar to those following amputation.

Osteosarcoma Research

Gene therapy may help dogs with osteosarcoma live longer and better, according to a recent study funded by Morris Animal Foundation of Englewood, Colorado. The canine patients all underwent amputation and chemotherapy, and X-rays confirmed osteosarcoma spread to their lungs. Researchers concluded the intravenous interleukin-2 gene therapy they received significantly increased survival time.

At AMC Cancer Research Center in Denver, a genetic study funded by Nestle Purina Co. and sixteen breed clubs is under way. Researchers want to determine which osteosarcoma-linked genetic abnormalities are inherited and which are sporadic. This knowledge eventually may help identify individuals or dog families where osteosarcoma is likely to develop.

At Colorado State University School of Veterinary Medicine and Biomedical Sciences, researchers are studying whether alendronate, the human drug Fosamax, can slow bone destruction in Irish Wolfhounds with osteosarcoma. In humans, the drug has been used to combat bone cancer and osteoporosis. In addition, Stephen Withrow, chief of clinical oncology at the school, has developed a technique involving sponges to deliver chemotherapy directly to osteosarcoma. The biodegradable sponges, soaked in chemotherapy drugs, are implanted at the tumor site. Dr. Withrow also has pioneered methods of bone regeneration and grafting.

Other researchers are investigating techniques to slow or cure osteosarcoma without amputation. A University of Missouri researcher is examining whether dogs who can't undergo amputation because of other health problems might benefit from a combination of carboplatin, a chemotherapy drug, and [153]Smarium-EDTMP, a bone-targeting drug. The drug cocktail would alleviate the pain, not cure the cancer.

Clinical trials have been done on drugs inhibiting the growth of new blood vessels for a variety of tumors in dogs. Researchers believe tumors starved of blood may regress and may be less likely to metastasize. In addition, a vitamin A derivative, 9-retinoic acid, has been shown to inhibit growth of canine osteosarcoma in the laboratory.

If It's Not Bone Cancer

Other cancers may cause lytic lesions in bone or similar swellings. Chondrosarcoma, a cartilage tumor, usually appears on flat bones, such as ribs and skull bones. Synovial cell sarcoma grows in the lining of the joint capsule, affecting both bones of the joint. Osteosarcoma doesn't cross joints.

Fungal infection may cause bone pain, but it won't cause lytic lesions. The infection results from inhalation of the fungus Coccidiodes immitis, native to the West and Southwest and the cause of valley fever in humans.

Skin Cancer

Dogs are prone to a great many classifiable lumps, cysts, growths, deposits, and tumors, the majority of which prove benign. However, some 20 percent are malignant or, rarely, become malignant. Because these growths are a normal part of the aging process, it is important to keep an eye on them and bring them to your veterinarian's attention.

Approximately one-third of all canine tumors are skin tumors. The good news is that the vast majority (about 80 percent) are benign and don't spread. Mast cell tumors account for about 8 to 20 percent of the skin tumors in dogs, making them the most frequently diagnosed malignant canine skin tumor, followed by squamous cell carcinomas (squamous cells make up most of the skin's outer layer), and certain melanomas.

The three most common types are lipomas, or fatty tumors; histiocytomas, or button tumors; and mast cell tumors, which are by far the most serious.

Fatty tumors, to which breeds like the Labrador Retriever are prone, are unsightly but not dangerous in most cases. Most dogs, if they get any at all, will have more than one. Most veterinarians aren't eager to remove them unless they inhibit the dog's quality of life—they can reach the size of baseballs—by growing in an armpit or the crook of a knee.

Histiocytomas are called buttons because that's what they resemble on the skin—raised, red, and often angry-looking "buttons" of rough tissue. Appearing in a spot where a dog is forced to leave them alone, they sometimes disappear without treatment. However, dog owners should never wait for the situation to resolve itself and should contact a veterinarian.

Mast cell tumors are very difficult to remove surgically. For this reason, veterinarians often recommend radiation and/or chemotherapy in conjunction with surgery, depending on the tumor's microscopic appearance at the time of the diagnosis. In its early stage, this cancer can often be successfully excised. Incompletely excised mast cell tumors often respond extremely well to radiation therapy.

Some mast cell tumors (MCTs) are smooth, firm, hairless red lumps on the skin surface. Others are rough and wart-like. Still other tumors are soft, hair-covered masses under the skin surface. Tumors may appear alone or in clusters. They can be slow-growing or fast-growing.

Both surgery and radiation therapy are considered "local" treatments that have little impact on metastatic disease. However, chemotherapy such as a basic, six-month course with a corticosteroid like prednisone, is useful when the disease has spread beyond the primary tumor. At this point, the prognosis is guarded, and treatment is focused on shrinking the tumors, slowing the further spread of disease, and maintaining a good quality of life for the dog.

In addition to surgery, radiation therapy, and chemotherapy, MCTs and other tumors can be treated with cryotherapy, which involves freezing the tumor with liquid nitrogen. However, its use is limited to certain very small tumors.

Mammary Cancer

The risks of this largely preventable cancer are directly correlated with whether and when a female dog has been spayed. (While extremely rare, this cancer also occurs in males.) Owners can virtually eliminate the risks of mammary cancer by spaying before a female first comes into season (when she can mate and become pregnant). If that is done, the risk of mammary cancer is almost zero. Even spaying before the fourth heat can help, according to Dr. Berg. "After the fourth heat, the sparing (of risk) effect is no longer present," he says.

While the exact cause of mammary cancer is unknown, female hormones play a part. Some mammary tumors have estrogen receptors, and the hormone estrogen promotes their growth. "The hormones definitely play a role, but that role hasn't been completely defined," Dr. Berg says. Similarly, the role of genetics isn't fully understood but is believed to play a part.

Poodles, along with Terriers, may have a slightly greater disposition to mammary tumors.

Mammary cancer, like most canine cancers, is closely associated with age. The average age of onset is ten years. "It's also true that purebred dogs tend to be more cancer-prone in general than mixed-breed dogs," Dr. Berg says.

Some veterinarians regard Poodles, Spaniels, Terriers, and German Shepherds as being slightly more predisposed to the disease than other breeds. Dogs at normal weight on their first birthday seem to be at less risk than overweight ones.

Female dogs have five pairs of mammary glands in what is called the mammary chain. The glands, which are often asymmetrical, should be soft and pliant if healthy. Don't panic if you find a lump in a mammary gland. About half of all the tumors are benign. However, all mammary lumps should be checked by a veterinarian.

"We use the 50/50/50 rule," Dr. Berg says. "If we see one hundred dogs with mammary tumors, about 50 percent will be benign, and 50 percent will be malignant. Of the malignant ones, about 50 percent of those will be fatal."

Even for malignancies—almost alone among the serious dog cancers—this one has a significant rate of cure, but only when caught early and the tumor is still localized.

Melanoma

Canine melanoma can occur in the skin (melanocytoma), but these tumors are usually benign. The most common and problematic tumors occur in the oral cavity. Other locations include the pads of the feet, the nail beds, lips, and behind and inside the eye.

Melanocytomas are prevalent among Standard and Miniature Schnauzers, Doberman Pinschers, Scottish Terriers, Irish and Gordon Setters, Viszlas, German Shepherds, and Golden Retrievers, with Schnauzers, Scotties and dogs with dark skin being at the greatest risk of developing malignant melanoma.

Signs include extremely bad breath, trouble chewing or food falling from the mouth while eating, bleeding, swelling on one side of the face, and weight loss. Average survival following diagnosis can range from six to eighteen months. In advanced stages of the disease, death usually occurs in three to six months.

Oral melanoma is much more common in dogs with dark pigmentation in their mouths. If you own such a dog, you need to be especially alert to unexplained oral swellings or signs of oral melanoma or what appears to be dental disease.

There is a theory that carcinogens may lodge on a dog's coat and become absorbed into oral tissues as a dog grooms. Fortunately, a major positive benefit of the growing emphasis on canine dental care is that this type of cancer can be diagnosed early.

"How we approach treatment depends on the location of the tumor," says Tufts' Dr. Barber. "In the front of the mouth, it can be more easily removed; toward the back of the mouth, we don't have much room to work. Many owners elect not to have disfiguring surgery done on their dog if it won't cure the disease."

Treatment is often palliative, that is, intended only to reduce suffering and eliminate the smell associated with oral melanoma.

"Radiation is pretty good for managing the disease," Dr. Barber says. "We give three to six doses of radiation because melanoma cells have the ability to repair the damage caused by small doses of radiation. Depending on how advanced the cancer is, this will make the dogs more comfortable and give them more time until the metastatic disease takes their lives."

Numerous researchers are studying treatment of oral melanoma:

■ Dr. Chieko Azuma, a Tufts clinical assistant professor who is board-certified in radiation oncology, is studying hypofractionated radiation—radiation given in very small, repeated doses—to treat oral melanoma.

■ New York City's Animal Medical Center, in collaboration with Memorial Sloan-Kettering Cancer Center, is working on a treatment that involves a vaccine. A DNA vaccine from another species is injected to tell the immune system to attack the tumor's cancer cells.

■ The University of Wisconsin-Madison is working on a vaccine for dogs with oral and digital melanoma.

Cancer Prevention

Of course, there is no magical diet, supplement, or vaccine that prevents cancer. But you can make some relatively simple choices to improve the odds.

Early spaying enormously reduces the risk of mammary cancer in females. Dogs spayed prior to initial estrus carry only half the risk of those spayed after the first but prior to the second heat cycle. Dogs spayed as young adults, or never spayed at all, have a risk factor increased by several hundred percent.

In male dogs, testicular cancer is common; neutering, obviously, eliminates that risk, and reduces the risk of both cancerous and non-cancerous prostate conditions, as well as anal cancer. If your dog is not neutered, do be aware that canine testicular cancer rarely spreads, and therefore has a relatively high rate of cure.

Pale-skinned dogs have a higher risk of skin cancer. A striking example of this risk is the Dalmatian, a breed currently high in popularity. Cancer is known to surround—but not enter—a Dalmatian's black spots. If you own a fair-skinned, short-haired breed, it would be best to limit your dog's sun exposure, especially at the times of day when the sun's rays are the most direct.

In Your Own Backyard

Occasionally, veterinary schools invite participation in cancer studies. They can be worthwhile if you live within driving distance of the veterinary hospital. However, Tufts' Dr. Berg advises that conventional cancer therapy often is the most appropriate.

"There are certainly opportunities to enter their dogs in studies, but quite often the best treatment is not far from where the owners live," he says.

Dr. Berg also cautions owners about information they finding surfing the Internet. "There's good and bad information on the Internet. Stick with Internet sites associated with veterinary schools, the Veterinary Cancer Society, or specialists in veterinary oncology."

Be Vigilant

While research continues, the best action owners can take is to be alert to the signs of cancer before it becomes advanced. If you find an unusual bump or lump, consult with your veterinarian. If the diagnosis is cancer, ask the veterinarian about treatment options and whether a specialist should be consulted. But above all, don't simply stay at home and worry.

"A common problem is that owners are afraid when they find a lump on their pet," Dr. Berg says. "It really needs to get checked out early so that it can be treated. Waiting until it spreads can complicate things and make a manageable situation difficult."

For More Information

Harrington Oncology Program
Foster Hospital for Small Animals
Tufts University School of Veterinary Medicine
200 Westboro Road
North Grafton, MA 01536
(508) 839-5395
www.tufts.edu/vet/sah/harrington.html

Veterinary Cancer Society
www.vetcancersociety.org

Morris Animal Foundation
45 Inverness Drive E.
Englewood, CO 80112
(800) 243-2345.
www.morrisanimalfoundation.org

AMC Cancer Research Center
1600 Pierce St.
Denver, CO 80214
(303) 239-3408
www.amc.org

Regional Veterinary Referral Center
6651 Backlick Road
Springfield, VA 22150
(703) 451-8900
www.vetreferralcenter.com ■

2

Heart Disease

*Early detection and treatment
often allow even dogs with serious disorders
to maintain a high quality of life.*

D ogs are bighearted animals. They're also animals who can suffer serious heart ailments. But if detected early enough, there are promising treatments available. Making sure your dog's heart is keeping the beat will not only prevent serious problems, it can greatly improve the quality of the dog's—and your—life. Knowing which dog breeds are most prone to heart disorders can help you in selecting a dog or in staying alert for the rise of possible problems.

The term "heart disease" refers to an abnormality in the functioning of the heart. Congenital heart disease is a malformation of the heart or of the great vessels—the major arteries and veins leading to and from the heart—and is present at birth. These malformations, which almost certainly have a genetic basis, are likely to become more severe with time.

Acquired heart disease develops as a result of environmental factors, though there may be a genetic predisposition to certain conditions.

If the disease is severe enough, heart failure will ultimately result. Failure occurs when the heart no longer functions well enough to meet the body's demands. This condition, if not caught early, eventually leads to death.

Heart failure has recognizable symptoms, but dogs affected with heart disease may also experience sudden death or catastrophic failure of the heart with little if any warning.

Offbeat Hearts

Irregular heartbeats (arrhythmias) occur when deviations in this perfectly timed impulse-conduction system lead to unsynchronized contractions. According to Dr. John Rush, professor and cardiologist at Tufts University School of Veterinary Medicine, "Arrhythmias are often caused by damage to heart muscle from preexisting heart ailments such as dilated cardiomyopathy [an enlarged, flabby, and weakly pumping heart] or valve disease." Systemic conditions that stress the heart—such as toxins in the bloodstream, brain disorders, and severe pancreatitis—can also cause arrhythmias.

Using a stethoscope, your veterinarian can detect abnormally fast or slow heartbeats (tachycardia and bradycardia, respectively). But only by evaluating an electrocardiogram (a recording of the heart's electrical activity) can a practitioner determine whence the arrhythmia originates.

Some arrhythmias are more dangerous than others. Arrhythmias that affect the upper chambers of the heart (supraventricular arrhythmias) can cause shortness of breath and fainting, but they tend not to be life threatening. On the other hand, arrhythmias that affect the heart's lower chambers (ventricular arrhythmias) are more serious and can result in sudden death.

Mild arrhythmias may not require treatment, and arrhythmias caused by systemic disease usually resolve after treatment of the underlying condition. However, patients with more severe arrhythmias—those that could cause collapse or death—need heart-specific treatment. Veterinarians usually treat bradycardia with medications that stimulate the heart to beat faster. These include terbutaline and propantheline (which modulate the nervous-system input to the heart) and aminophylline (which acts directly on the heart muscle to increase the heart rate). Unfortunately, in some patients, the heart muscle stops responding to drug therapy after a period of time. "Such patients might benefit from implantation of an artificial pacemaker," says Dr. Rush.

*Veterinarians treat tachycardias with drugs that slow
the heart rate. These include propranolol (which blocks
the effect of the heart-stimulating hormone adrenaline),
procainamide (which directly depresses heart-muscle
contractions), and calcium-channel blockers (which
decrease the rate of electrical impulses).*

BREEDS AND HEART DISEASE

Disorder	Breeds Commonly Affected	Treatment Options
Aortic Stenosis	Bernese Mountain Dog Bouvier de Flandres Boxer Bull Terrier German Shepherd Golden Retriever Newfoundland Rottweiler	Surgery has had very limited success. Balloon angioplasty may correct some cases. Beta blocks and other drug therapies are the most frequent treatment.
Patent Ductus Arteriosus	Collie English Springer Spaniel German Shepherd Maltese Poodle Pomeranian Shetland Sheepdog	Surgical correction is feasible and recommended to avoid future complications
Pulmonic Stenosis	Beagle Chihuahua English Bulldog Fox Terrier Miniature Schnauzer Samoyed	Asymptomatic dogs may need no treatment. Various surgical options including balloon valvuloplasty. Beta blocker therapy sometimes effective.
Ventricular Septal Defect	English Bulldog Keeshond	Only corrective surgical option is open heart. Smaller defects may not require treatment but should be monitored.

Suspicions of Congenital Heart Disease

Murmurs are usually the earliest sign of a congenital disorder and may appear long before your dog exhibits any other symptoms. The good news: early detection enhances a dog's chances of being successfully treated and living a normal, healthy life. Your veterinarian can often detect the cardiac murmurs associated with these diseases during the course of a routine examination.

A murmur means the dog's heart has a leaky valve, most often due to age-related deterioration but sometimes due to developmental defects or abnormal shunting of blood.

Lesions can form in the first half of life, as early as age two or three. Among Cavalier King Charles Spaniels—a particularly susceptible breed—dogs occasionally develop a heart murmur even before the first birthday, says Dr. Jim Ross, a cardiologist and distinguished professor at Tufts University School of Veterinary Medicine.

A heart murmur doesn't automatically command treatment or necessarily mean that a dog has significant heart disease. If the heart is of normal size, not enlarged, and no other symptoms are observed, then treatment often isn't needed.

Early signs of a worsening condition that needs further attention may include reduced exercise tolerance, indicated by labored breathing after minimal exercise or a reduction in your dog's level of activity; syncope (fainting); and lethargy. These symptoms may be more apparent in active dogs because they are continually placing higher demands on their circulatory system.

As the condition advances or heart failure ensues, your dog may experience a reduced appetite and weight loss, and his or her tongue and gums may exhibit a bluish tinge. Fluid builds up in the lungs or abdomen as the efficiency of the circulatory system decreases. Congestion in the lungs leads to dyspnea, or difficulty breathing at rest, and wheezing. Dogs experiencing dyspnea will often sit with their elbows turned out in an effort to ease breathing. Because the condition worsens when the dog is at rest, pacing or restlessness at night may also indicate congestion in the lungs. An affected dog may have a cough, but that could also signal pulmonary disease and should not be the first obvious symptom of heart disease or failure. Distension of the abdomen is another sign of fluid retention.

An extremely rapid or slow heart rate may be a warning that something is amiss. Dr. Ross advises owners to monitor their dogs'

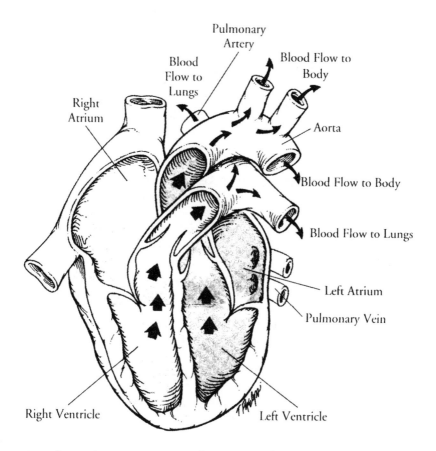

One of your dog's most amazing features is its beautifully synchronized heartbeat. Specialized "wiring" embedded in your dog's heart muscle conducts electrical impulses, creating an orchestra of muscle contractions that pump blood hither and yon.

heart rates at home. A normal rate in resting adult dogs ranges from 75 to 120 beats per minute; contact your veterinarian if your dog's resting heart rate is consistently higher than 120 beats per minute.

Certain breeds are more prone to exhibit malformations than others. Mixed breeds seem to experience a much lower incidence of these disorders, and affected individuals almost always have one of the indicated breeds in their pedigree. Heart disease can also cause a stunting of growth, so the runt of the litter may well be suffering from a congenital disorder. If you are particularly fond of one of these breeds or fall in love with the runt of the litter, be on the lookout for early signs of cardiac irregularity in your pet.

Chronic Valve Disease

Endocardiosis, or chronic valve disease, is by far the most common cardiac disease in dogs and the most frequent cause of congestive heart failure. More precisely termed myxomatous atrioventricular valvular degeneration, it's a slowly progressing disease in which heart valves degenerate. Veterinarians don't know its cause in dogs, though it seems to have a genetic component. They also don't know how to prevent it.

Older, smaller dogs are more likely to be diagnosed with chronic valve disease, but it also occurs in large breeds. About 60 percent of dogs over the age of eight years are affected.

The disease is more common in males than females. Among the small breeds in which it is more commonly seen are Cavalier King Charles Spaniels, Dachshunds, Miniature Poodles, Shetland Sheepdogs, Lhasa Apsos, Cocker Spaniels, Schnauzers, and Yorkshire Terriers.

With proper treatment, some dogs can live for years with degenerative valve disease while others develop congestive heart failure in a matter of months after a murmur is discovered. But

A stethoscope reveals the sound of blood moving backward in a leaky valve.

ANDREW CUNNINGHAM, TUSVM

what optimal treatment for chronic valve disease is remains a challenge.

"A variety of drugs and diets have been developed to manage the disease," says Dr. Matthew W. Miller, associate professor of cardiology at Texas A&M University College of Veterinary Medicine. "However, little research has been done to identify the cause of the valvular degeneration."

He says that if the cause could be identified and treated, "then the disease could be slowed or reversed." Until that time, management of congestive heart failure remains the cornerstone of therapy for valvular disease, he says.

Hearts Apart

The cause and progression of heart disease in dogs is markedly different from the cause and progression in people, though both species (especially older members) are subject to heart failure.

In people, heart failure most commonly arises from:

- *severe hypertension (abnormally high blood pressure)*

- *coronary artery disease (blockages of the blood vessels that supply blood to the heart muscle)*

In dogs, heart failure is most often triggered by:

- *dilated cardiomyopathy*

- *heart valve disease*

Taking Heart

Although no cure exists for canine congestive heart failure (CHF), Food and Drug Administration (FDA) approval of enalapril maleate for use in dogs promises a more comfortable life for afflicted animals.

Congestive heart failure occurs when the heart's valves malfunction or its muscles weaken.

Consequently, blood pools, and its fluid component (serum) leaks out of blood vessels into body cavities. This causes the swelling (edema) characteristic of CHF. Enalapril, originally developed to treat high blood pressure in humans, dilates blood vessels to help reduce the heart's workload, thus alleviating some of CHF's most serious symptoms.

Unfortunately, many dogs do not display CHF symptoms, such as coughing (caused by edema in the lungs), weight loss, and fatigue until the disease has progressed significantly.

Traditionally, veterinarians have treated CHF with heart-strengthening drugs such as digoxin and with diuretics, which induce the kidneys to excrete excess fluids. "Diuretics, however, don't make it easier for the heart to pump blood," says Dr. John Rush, a cardiologist and professor at Tufts University School of Veterinary Medicine and a participant in clinical trials of enalapril. Used in conjunction with diuretics, enalapril interrupts a naturally occurring hormone-enzyme reaction. The result: dilated blood vessels that decrease strain on the heart, and increased fluid removal by the kidneys, relieving edema.

Prior to enalapril's approval, veterinarians treated CHF with other vessel-opening (vasodilating) drugs designed for people. Some of these caused side effects; others stimulated vasodilation without inhibiting the underlying chemical reaction. "With congestive heart failure treatment, it's better to directly interfere with the mechanisms that cause the problem," says Dr. Rush. Enalapril (trade-named Enacard by Merck & Co.) is the only such FDA-approved drug for dogs.

Although enalapril eases life for dogs with CHF and often restores lost stamina, its life-extending potential is difficult to predict. "With CHF, it's impossible to make accurate prognoses of how much longer a dog receiving any treatment will live," says Dr. Rush. "But having an approved drug that is safe and proven effective in dogs is tremendous."

Categories of Heart Disease

The canine heart, like the human heart, is a four-chambered organ consisting of two atria and two ventricles. Veins carry blood to the heart and arteries carry it away. Valves leading out of the heart and from the atria to the ventricles ensure that the flow of blood is strictly one way.

The right atrium receives the "used" blood from the body and pumps it to the right ventricle, which sends it through the pulmonary arteries to the lungs for oxygenation.

Once reinvigorated, blood returns to the heart via the pulmonary veins to the left atrium. From here the "fresh" blood is delivered throughout the body's arteries. To ensure that stale and fresh blood do not mix, septa, or walls of cardiac tissue, separate the left chambers from the right.

Congenital heart defects can be classified broadly into:

■ valvular dysplasia, or malformation,
■ septal defects, and
■ constriction of the vessels leaving the heart.

A malformed cardiac valve will not close fully, resulting in a backwash: for example, blood may flow back into the left atrium due to a leaky mitral valve between that chamber and the ventricle. The severity of these conditions varies and medical intervention may be indicated, but many dogs live relatively normal lives with little or no treatment. In a disorder called ventricular septal defect ("hole in the heart disease"), the septum between the ventricles does not form completely, allowing stale and fresh blood to mix.

If the defect is large enough, it can prevent a significant amount of oxygenated blood from reaching its destination. The third set of developmental miscues involves a narrowing of the aorta or pulmonary artery at or around the valve (aortic or pulmonic stenosis), forcing the ventricles to work harder to pump the blood.

Another relatively common defect that does not fit neatly into any of the categories described above is patent ductus arteriosus. In dogs exhibiting this disorder, a shunt that connects the aorta and pulmonary artery in the fetus fails to close once the puppy is born. This defect also permits mixing of stale and fresh blood, leading to a shortage of oxygen-rich blood in the body.

With all of these conditions, the physiological consequences are ultimately the same—circulation is compromised and the muscle of the heart must work harder to meet the body's oxygen needs. The severity and progression of the defect and the overall health of your dog will determine whether this increase in stress will lead to heart failure.

Diagnosis

Cardiac Auscultation

Once you suspect the presence of a congenital heart disorder, your first step is to have a specialist listen to your dog's heart with a stethoscope (cardiac auscultation).

Each disorder is associated with a specific cardiac murmur. With auscultation alone, a certified cardiologist often is able to distinguish these pathological murmurs from "innocent" murmurs that often show up in, for example, young or active dogs and dogs suffering from anemia. Your veterinarian may be able to recommend a cardiologist; otherwise, contact either the American Veterinary Medicine Association (AVMA) or affiliated state organization to receive a listing of cardiologists in your area.

Chest X-ray

When a suspicious murmur is detected, a chest X-ray can offer more information about the type and severity of the disorder by revealing hypertrophy, or enlargement of the overworked heart muscle, and changes in the degree of pulmonary vascularity, both of which are associated with particular disorders.

The only risk involved is the use of a mild sedative on dogs who otherwise cannot be kept still enough to complete the procedure.

Electrocardiography (EKG or ECG)

The cardiologist may also decide to perform an EKG to look for heart enlargement and detect arrhythmias. EKGs are not a definitive tool for diagnosing congenital diseases, but they are noninvasive and relatively inexpensive, and offer another avenue for gathering useful information about your dog's condition.

Echocardiography With Doppler

Echocardiography with Doppler uses ultrasound to produce moving pictures of the dog's heart and to observe the speed, amount, and direction of blood flow through the chambers and great vessels. This procedure is now the preferred method for reaching a definitive diagnosis of congenital heart disease. It is noninvasive and relatively risk free. Because sedatives affect the circulatory system, they are used only as a last resort when obtaining an echocardiograph.

Cardiac Catheterization

Before echocardiography came along, the only definitive test for congenital heart disease was cardiac catheterization. This procedure is still used in a number of cases because it remains the most precise of the tools and may sometimes be used for both diagnosis and treatment. During the procedure, the cardiologist introduces a catheter into a vein and guides it into the heart itself. With the catheter it is possible to sample blood in each chamber for oxygen content, record pressures, and inject dye into the vessels to trace its movement through the vessels and the chambers (angiocardiography). This last option is helpful when surgery is under consideration because it provides a clearer "picture" of the malformation than does the echocardiograph.

With certain disorders, it is possible to perform treatment on the spot. If catheterization confirms a patent ductus arteriosis, for example, a coil may be placed on the catheter and inserted into the ductus, effectively closing this undesirable shunt. In cases of pulmonic stenosis, a balloon may be carried on the tip of the catheter and inflated at the affected valve in an attempt to break down the narrowing (balloon valvuloplasty). This invasive procedure is the riskiest of the diagnostic tools. There are the usual risks associated with anesthesia. The catheter may also trigger arrhythmia or your dog may have an allergic reaction to the dye. And, there are slight risks of perforating the heart of a small puppy or causing bleeding. Cost depends on the complexity of the procedures.

The Threat of Blood Clots

When a veterinarian tells you your dog is suffering thromboembolism, be aware that the condition probably didn't crop up overnight. The formation of blood-obstructing clots generally relates to an underlying medical condition.

Almost all thromboembolism results from venostasis, or slow blood flow; injury to a vein or artery; or hypercoagulability, an abnormal tendency of the blood to form clots, says Tufts' Dr. Ross.

A thromboembolism is the obstruction of a blood vessel by an embolus, or blood clot, which has broken away from a thrombus, a fibrinous coagulation of blood. Like a leaf in a stream, the embolus travels as far as possible through the bloodstream, until it reaches a vessel too small to pass. There it lodges, blocking the blood behind it. Without flowing blood to bring nutrients and carry away wastes, tissues die.

Embolisms in dogs are rarer than in cats. They sometimes resolve themselves with no aftereffects, especially in the case of dogs with pulmonary thromboembolism related to heartworm treatment, Dr. Ross says. "In many dogs, when you kill the worms, they all embolize in the lungs. But they tend to absorb the emboli fairly rapidly."

Pulmonary thromboembolism not related to heartworm treatment can be more difficult to identify and treat. Although a veterinarian may order chest X-rays, the pictures may not show the clot. Other scanning tests can be done to show whether blood flow has become static in the lungs.

Kidney conditions—including glomerulonephritis and renal dysplasia—may lead to thromboembolism as the kidneys become less able to filter certain clotting-related proteins from the blood. Infective endocarditis, a bacterial or fungal infection of the heart's lining, can also affect the heart valves and cause emboli to form. Other associated diseases can include immune-related hemolytic anemia and Cushing's disease. But Dr. Ross warns owners of dogs with these diseases and conditions not to panic. "Even when we're looking at Cushing's, the vast majority of dogs don't develop thromboembolism."

Treatment

Dr. Ross uses several criteria to determine treatment once a diagnosis has been reached:

■ current physiological reaction to the disorder, including hypertrophy, arrhythmias, and elevated pressure

■ natural history of the disease

■ symptoms and the owner's level of anxiety about those symptoms

■ availability of a good palliative option

In general, congenital heart disease leads to reduced longevity. But if corrective surgery is successful, then a dog's chances of leading a normal life are greatly improved. However, surgery is not feasible in many cases, either because effective procedures have not

> 66 THE GOAL OF ANY TREATMENT,
> WHETHER IT INVOLVES CORRECTING
> THE DEFECT OR SIMPLY AMELIORATING
> THE SYMPTOMS, IS TO AVOID HEART
> FAILURE OR SUDDEN DEATH. 99

yet been developed or because cost and logistics are prohibitive. The disorder may also be mild enough that the best option is to do nothing but monitor the dog's condition.

The goal of any treatment, whether it involves correcting the defect or simply ameliorating the symptoms, is to avoid heart failure or sudden death. Once a dog suffering from an uncorrectable disorder enters heart failure, the animal's life expectancy is no more than six months, and treatment will be aimed at maintaining quality of life.

About Open-Heart Surgery

In the simplest terms, open-heart surgery means that surgeons make an incision in the heart. Because the heart must remain still and free of blood for them to work, they usually give medication to stop the heart's beating, while a bypass machine diverts blood away from the heart and lungs. The blood runs from the body's major veins into the machine, where it is oxygenated, and returned through the major arteries. The machine acts as a surrogate for the heart and lungs while surgeons repair the damaged organ.

Open-heart surgery can repair damaged mitral valves and correct conditions such as congenital heart defects. Mitral valve disease causes a leakage of blood in the heart and makes the organ less efficient. It's thought to affect as many as a third of dogs over the age of ten. With open-heart surgery, cardiologists can either repair the damaged valve or replace it with a prosthetic valve.

> *Tufts University School of Veterinary Medicine is among a handful of places in the country that perform open-heart surgery on dogs. Says Dr. John Berg, veterinary surgeon and chair of Tufts University School of Veterinary Medicine's Department of Clinical Science: "Dogs with severe mitral valve disease can be very limited in their ability to exercise and often die prematurely of congestive heart failure. Although valve replacement is risky, it is often the only option that provides hope for a normal quality of life and normal life-span."*

Surgical Approaches

In cases where the untreated disorder is likely to lead to dangerous complications and corrective surgery has a high rate of success, surgery is the obvious choice. For example, Dr. Ross recommends that all dogs diagnosed with patent ductus arteriosus undergo the catheter and coil procedure discussed above. The success rate is high and the cost is not astronomical, though it may run several thousand dollars. Also relatively inexpensive is balloon valvuloplasty, a procedure that has been used with some success for pulmonic stenosis and in certain cases of aortic stenosis.

There are other surgical approaches, including open-heart surgery, but their success rates are not as encouraging, and cost— many thousands of dollars— may often be prohibitive.

When corrective surgery is not feasible, the best advice may be to treat the disorder's symptoms to extend longevity and maintain a comfortable quality of life for the dog. For example, the body's response to insufficient cardiac output is vasoconstriction, a narrowing of the blood vessels that restores blood pressure to a "normal" level. In the short term, this response is appropriate but in the long run it may hasten the onset of failure by requiring the heart to work harder.

A class of drugs known as vasodilators allow the blood vessels to expand, thus reducing the strain on the heart. Beta blockers slow the heart rate and allow the heart to pump less forcefully, with the same result.

However, beta blockers may also precipitate heart failure in weakened individuals, so their use must be carefully monitored. The administration of diuretics is a relatively simple therapy for managing pulmonary edema, or retention of fluid in the lungs, a condition associated with right-sided heart disorders.

This dog was the first to have open-heart surgery at Tufts..

Keeping Pace

Using "spares" designed for humans, veterinarians have successfully implanted artificial pacemakers in dogs with irregular heartbeats. But because the supply is limited and the cost relatively high, not all dogs who might benefit from a pacemaker receive one.

"A pacemaker consists of a battery-powered pulse generator connected to a lead wire," says Dr. Rush. Veterinarians typically implant the pulse generator under the skin in the dog's neck and guide the lead wire through veins into the right ventricle, where the pulses initiate proper muscle contractions.

Implantation, however, is not the end of the story. Pacemaker batteries generally last from two to five years, so young dogs may need replacements. It's also important to frequently monitor dogs with pacemakers so veterinarians can identify and fix any problems.

Dietary Strategies

No one knows what role, if any, diet can play in preventing canine heart disease. However, veterinary nutritionists and cardiologists are working on dietary strategies to help treat existing heart disease.

For dogs with heart disease, veterinarians often prescribe exercise modification and medication—diuretics to increase fluid excretion from the kidneys and vasodilating drugs that enlarge blood vessels to reduce heart strain. Another common veterinary recommendation is a low-sodium (low-salt) diet, although there are no controlled studies proving the effectiveness of this approach. The first study investigating the benefits of a low-salt diet in dogs with heart disease is now under way at Tufts.

The premise is that dogs with heart disease have a harder time ridding their bodies of sodium than their healthy counterparts. And because excess sodium increases water retention, the body's total fluid volume rises. The already struggling heart must now work even harder to pump surplus fluid. Current thinking on low-sodium diets is that they counteract fluid retention, which allows veterinarians to prescribe lower doses of diuretics.

However, according to Dr. Lisa Freeman, Tufts associate professor and veterinary nutritionist, not all canine cardiac patients need—or benefit from—severely sodium-restricted "cardiac diets." (Still, avoid high-sodium dog food, processed people foods, and lunch meat in your dog's diet if he or she has heart disease.) "When trying to establish an appropriate diet, it's important to take into account the severity of the individual dog's disease and the medications it's taking," says Dr. Freeman.

Many canine cardiac patients suffer loss of appetite, perhaps due in part to the sometimes "blah" taste of low-sodium food or a sudden change in cuisine. Certain heart medications can also lead to anorexia, as can changes in hormones and hormonelike substances associated with heart disease.

Two such substances, tumor necrosis factor (TNF) and interleukin 1 (IL1), have been isolated in human patients with heart failure, and both are known to cause anorexia and loss of muscle tissue. A study conducted by Dr. Freeman showed that supplementing canine diets with fish oil containing omega-3 fatty acids lowers IL1 levels and can help increase appetite and muscle mass in some dogs with heart failure.

Taurine (an amino acid) and carnitine (an amino-acid-like substance) are two other nutrients that may prove useful in treating a certain subset of canine heart patients. One study found low levels of taurine in a small number of Cocker Spaniels with dilated cardiomyopathy (a condition characterized by enlarged, flabby, and weakly pumping heart muscles). In veterinary clinical experience, however, taurine supplementation has not been very effective in treating the majority of dogs with cardiomyopathy.

Carnitine facilitates the transport of fatty acids (an important energy source) into heart muscle. Carnitine deficiencies have been linked to cardiomyopathy in children—and, on the canine front, to cardiomyopathy in one particular family of Boxers. While these affected Boxers responded well to carnitine supplementation, most dogs treated clinically with carnitine have shown only modest or no improvement. Boxers with dilated cardiomyopathy have ventricles with less or minimal dilation compared with other dogs, and only the left ventricle weakens rather than both ventricles.

Always consult your veterinarian before altering your dog's menu and be sure to introduce new food gradually over four to five days. Doing so will keep gastrointestinal upsets to a minimum and help your dog adjust to the taste of the new food.

More About Dilated Cardiomyopathy

Dilated cardiomyopathy (DCM) causes the heart muscle to enlarge and function improperly. The disease most often arises from unknown causes.

Some breeds, such as Doberman Pinschers, seem genetically predisposed to it. A few dogs may develop DCM because of dietary deficiencies; viral infections, such as parvovirus and Lyme disease; and some medications, such as the cancer-fighting drug doxorubicin.

"There have been no big breakthroughs in treating dilated cardiomyopathy," says Dr. Ross. "Probably we'll have some genetic breakthroughs," he says, noting that more than half of Dobermans may carry a gene related to DCM. Giant and large breeds are most often affected; however, American and English Cocker Spaniels also develop the disease. The incidence is most common among males and dogs ages four to ten years.

Environment

Finally, once a dog is experiencing heart failure, restriction of exercise and a home environment free of stress and hard work such as climbing stairs will increase the animal's comfort level and enable him or her to respond more favorably to corrective or palliative therapy.

Dr. Ross emphasizes that even in cases where the defect may be successfully corrected, all dogs diagnosed with these heritable disorders should be spayed or neutered. The vigilance of owners, breeders, and their veterinarians may eventually save future canine generations from these troublesome, and potentially deadly, diseases. ■

3

Kidney Disease

*Kidneys maintain the delicate balance
of life-sustaining chemicals in your
dog's blood and pump out wastes.*

Shaped like the run-of-the-mill beans bearing their name, your dog's two kidneys are anything but ordinary. They help regulate your dog's blood pressure, activate vitamin D (a regulator of calcium and phosphorus metabolism), and produce erythropoietin (a hormone that stimulates red blood cell production). Considering how many essential functions your dog's kidneys perform, you should know how these organs work—and what can happen if they don't.

The kidney's filtering and fluid-balancing work occurs in microscopic tubes called nephrons. Nephrons are versatile but not invincible. If any part of a nephron is damaged—due to infection, poisons, genetic predisposition, trauma, or aging—the entire nephron stops functioning. Fortunately, even if your dog loses some nephrons, the surviving nephrons have the capacity to grow larger (hypertrophy) to compensate. If damage to nephrons occurs gradually and the surviving nephrons have enough time to hypertrophy, a kidney can continue to function with as few as 25 percent of its original nephrons.

Kidney Failure

However, when the number of functioning nephrons dips below 25 percent or when nephron damage occurs too suddenly for the remaining nephrons to compensate, kidney failure occurs. There

It's easy for owners to overlook kidney disease signs such as lethargy and depression because they seem so mild.

are two types of kidney failure. Acute kidney failure is an abrupt loss of function that is sometimes but not always reversible. Chronic kidney failure is an irreversible loss of function that occurs gradually over months or years.

"Because kidneys are so hard-working, dogs with chronic kidney disease usually don't show signs—loss of appetite, excessive drinking and urinating, lethargy, and vomiting—until the problem is well advanced," says Dr. Linda Ross, associate professor and veterinary internist with Tufts University School of Veterinary Medicine. Unfortunately, the standard kidney-function blood tests—blood urea nitrogen (BUN) and serum creatinine—are unable to detect problems until about 75 percent of the kidney's functional filters are destroyed. Glomerular filtration rate (GFR) tests measure the filtering efficiency of the glomerulus, an integral part of each nephron. While GFR tests can identify kidney problems earlier, they can require immobilizing a dog and hooking it up to a urine-collecting catheter for several hours.

Failing kidneys can't adequately clear the blood of urea (a nitrogen-containing byproduct of protein metabolism) and creatinine (a chemical byproduct of muscle exertion). Consequently, when kidneys fail, the circulating blood contains abnormally high levels of these wastes. Other blood components normally kept in check by the kidneys, such as phosphorus, calcium, sodium, potassium, and chloride, also rise or fall abnormally. Healthy kidneys produce concentrated urine that is relatively protein-free; failing kidneys may also produce extremely diluted urine or urine that contains too much protein.

A diagnosis of kidney failure is not necessarily a death sentence, but it's impossible for veterinarians to determine at the outset the dog's chances for getting better. Rather, practitioners must test blood and urine frequently during treatment to evaluate how well surviving nephrons are responding. It's a good sign if test results swing back toward normal within the first forty-eight to seventy-two hours of therapy.

Initial test results can be remarkably similar for both forms of kidney failure, so "the diagnostic challenge is to determine whether the dog has acute or chronic kidney failure," says Dr. Ross. Making the distinction between chronic and acute failure is crucial because the prognosis and duration of treatment for the two types of kidney disease are different, although some treatment procedures may be similar.

Signs of Kidney Disease

With kidney disease, your dog becomes less alert, loses his or her appetite, and may vomit. Take your dog to the veterinarian if the animal shows any of the following signs that sometimes (but not always) point to kidney disease:

Chronic Failure
■ *Increased thirst and urine volume*

■ *Weight loss*

■ *Weakness and exercise intolerance*

■ *Tendency to bleed or bruise easily*

Acute Failure
■ *Dehydration (To test for this, gently pull the skin away from your dog's middle. If the skin does not immediately spring back, the dog may be dehydrated.)*

■ *Stiff-legged gait and arched back (signs of painful kidneys)*

■ *Little or no urine production*

Acute Failure

Acute kidney failure (AKF) occurs so suddenly that surviving nephrons don't have time to hypertrophy. This abrupt failure can occur if the kidney is damaged by an infection such as leptospirosis (a bacterial disease); harmful substances such as antifreeze and rat poison; or certain medications, including some antibiotics and chemotherapy drugs.

Vaccines can protect against most, but not all, strains of the Leptospira bacterium that causes leptospirosis. But bacteria other than Leptospira can also cause kidney infections, invading vulnerable parts of the urinary tract (the bladder, for example) and then migrating to the kidneys. Fortunately, if detected early enough, many bacterial infections can be treated effectively with antibiotics, and dogs often recover completely.

Chronic Failure

Chronic kidney failure (CKF) is the most common form of kidney disease in dogs and among the most common causes of death in older dogs. Some breeds, including Cocker Spaniels, Samoyeds, and Bull Terriers, are genetically predisposed to chronic kidney failure.

CKF progresses over a period of years and often goes unnoticed by even the most vigilant owners. When signs finally appear, the

Excessive thirst, one of the symptoms of kidney failure, can indicate many other diseases and conditions.

disease is often well advanced. Nevertheless, with proper treatment and careful long-term monitoring, some dogs with chronic kidney failure live comfortably for years after diagnosis.

Dogs with CKF tend to produce large amounts of dilute urine (polyuria) because there aren't enough healthy nephrons to properly channel excess water back into the bloodstream. Consequently, CKF dogs drink lots of water (a condition called polydipsia) to maintain the right volume of internal fluids.

CKF can be the sequel to acute kidney failure or the result of insidious diseases that slowly destroy nephrons. One such long-term condition is glomerulonephritis, in which immune-system proteins damage the glomerulus (the tuft of blood vessels at the entrance to the nephron). But, more often than not, it's impossible to identify the exact cause of CKF.

Ingested Poisons

Kidney function may shut down if your dog ingests ethylene-glycol-based antifreeze, which forms crystals inside the dog's nephrons. If a dog gets to the veterinarian quickly enough, hemodialysis may remove ethylene glycol from the blood before it breaks down and does damage, Dr. Ross says. However, few veterinary hospitals offer this treatment. (Tufts is among them.) The treatment commonly requires commitment to the dialysis equipment three times a week at a cost of eight thousand dollars or more for several weeks.

Another potentially lethal substance is rat poison. If a dog eats rat poison containing calciferol (a form of vitamin D), the calciferol pushes up the dog's calcium level, causing mineral deposits, inflammation, and other damage within the kidneys.

Dialysis and Antibiotics

Intravenous fluid therapy can temporarily help dogs who have acute or chronic kidney failure. Your veterinarian may prescribe medications such as calcitriol to help regulate blood levels of calcium and phosphorus, or erythropoietin to boost red blood cell production.

How They Work

The kidneys are nestled behind the ribs near the spine, where they're protected from ruptures or tears. Here's a summary of how the kidney works:

1. *Blood delivered to the kidney via the renal artery passes through smaller blood vessels to the nephrons.*

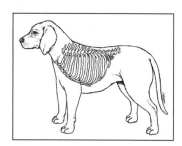

2. *Water, urea and creatinine (waste products), glucose (primary energy source), amino acids (building blocks of proteins), and electrolytes (electrically charged particles that regulate the flow of water across cell membranes) move from the bloodstream through the ball-shaped glomerulus and into the nephron's tubules. The glomerulus prevents blood cells and most proteins from entering the tubules.*

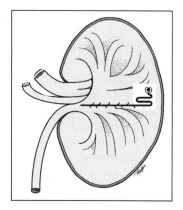

3. *As this mix flows through the nephron's convoluted tubes, the life-sustaining constituents (such as glucose, amino acids, and any water and electrolytes needed by the body) are reabsorbed into the blood vessels surrounding the nephron. From there, the "recycled" substances enter the renal vein for the journey back out to the body.*

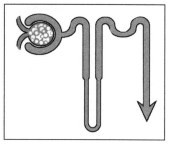

4. *Waste products and excess water and electrolytes flow into the collecting duct, through the ureter, and on to the bladder for excretion as urine.*

Veterinarians sometimes resort to more intensive treatments such as dialysis (artificial blood filtering). However, the process is labor- and technology-intensive and therefore very expensive. Dialysis requires several hours of treatment several times a week on an ongoing basis.

Ironically, treatment for some nonkidney diseases can jeopardize the kidneys. Although most antibiotics cause no harm to the kidneys, dogs on certain antibiotics—gentamicin, for example—must be closely monitored because of potential damage to nephrons. Cisplatin, an anticancer drug, and amphotericin B, a drug for serious fungal infections, also can cause acute kidney damage. In general, before you decide on a course of treatment for any condition, ask your veterinarian about the benefits and risks of all available options.

Transplants

About 30 dogs have undergone kidney transplants at the University of California at Davis, the premier canine renal transplant program in the country. A few other dogs have had them at other veterinary schools. However, feline kidney transplants number in the hundreds. Few of the dog recipients survived; the success rate among cats is definitely higher.

The reason: dogs have more difficulty accepting transplanted kidneys. While cats can receive donor kidneys from almost any other cat, canine donors and recipients must be more carefully matched. Dogs have seven blood types and major and minor tissue types, leading to many variations. Cats, on the other hand, have only three blood types, and 80 percent to 90 percent of them have the same type, making it much easier to match feline donors and recipients.

"The most likely reason why dogs reject kidney transplants is that they are much more genetically diverse than cats, although it is possible that there is also some difference in their immune systems," Dr. Ross says. "Kidneys from dogs that are related are strongly preferred."

At the University of Liverpool in England, researchers are studying methods of typing and matching canine tissues so that donor matches can be made among unrelated dogs. This could help stop organ rejection caused by genetic diversity. Currently, no method exists for matching the patient and donor. Veterinarians try to raise the odds of a match by moving kidneys from related dogs. Morris Animal Foundation, based in Englewood, Colo., is funding the research.

Even among related dogs, rejection remains a barrier to success-ful transplants. In fact, rejection was such an issue for dogs that an earlier UC Davis program that began in 1984 involved only twelve transplant patients and lasted only ten years. All the patients were given the immune-suppressive drug cyclosporine to fight the body's natural inclination to battle foreign bodies, but the treatment was successful with only one dog.

The program began again in 1999. "Our biggest challenge now is not rejection but mainly complications of hypercoagulability" of the blood, says Dr. Lynda Bernsteen, director of clinical transplant ser-vices at the college. "Most of the dogs that didn't make it [since the program resumed] have died early in the perioperative period, three to fourteen days after surgery, from blood clots forming, especially in the lungs."

And at Auburn University, researchers funded by Morris are look-ing at bone-marrow transplants to suppress dogs' kidney rejection. They hope to learn whether a bone-marrow transplant alone or tem-porary suppression of immune responses or some combination will increase acceptance of transplanted kidneys.

"The theory is that by establishing the bone marrow of the donor in the recipient dog, the recipient dog's immune system will 'see' the transplanted kidney as 'self' and not as foreign," says Dr. Michael Tillson, one of the Auburn researchers. "This is called immunologic tolerance and could allow us to eliminate the need for long-term immunosuppressive drugs in dogs after transplantation."

The UC Davis Transplant Program

University of California at Davis veterinarians advise owners to seek transplantation as soon after diagnosis of renal failure as possible. UC Davis will not do a transplant as a final effort to save a sick dog.

To be considered, the dog must be healthy except for renal failure. The animal must pass fifteen physical screening tests that his or her regular veterinarian can administer, with results faxed to the university. The dog must be free of signs of most cardiac disease, urinary tract infection, inflammatory bowel disease, diabetes and Cushing's disease, poor body condition, and unruly temperament.

The school encourages owners to provide kidney donors. Donor dogs should be younger than six years old and about the same size or slightly bigger than the recipient, though they need not be of the same breed. Donors must pass eight screening tests to ensure they're free of systemic illnesses.

If the school lines up the donor, the owner of the transplant recipient must pay for all screening tests. Because UC Davis donor dogs come from shelters, the school requires the owner to adopt the donor after the surgery.

Learn more details about the program by visiting or contacting Dr. Lynda Bernsteen, director of the clinical transplant service, at: University of California, Davis Veterinary Medical Teaching Hospital 1 Shields Avenue, Davis, CA 95616-8747. Phone: (530) 752-1393; Web site: **www.vetmed.ucdavis.edu**.

At Home: Ongoing Treatment

The key to ongoing CKF treatment takes place at home, where owners can take several steps to help their dogs. Make sure a dog with CKF always has access to fresh water. To encourage the dog to drink and eat, maintain a steady, stress-free daily routine. Stressed-out dogs have been known to stop drinking and eating, further jeopardizing kidney function.

Dietary management can also help your dog, but according to Dr. Lisa Freeman, associate professor and veterinary nutritionist at Tufts, "you must treat each dog as an individual." Commercial therapeutic diets available from veterinarians may benefit your dog, but not every dog with kidney disease needs such a diet.

Studies suggest that feeding your dog a diet low in phosphorus may help slow the progression of kidney failure by reducing mineral deposits in the kidneys. And while there's no conclusive proof that low-protein diets slow CKF in dogs, low-protein diets do generate fewer nitrogenous wastes, high levels of which can cause nausea and vomiting in dogs with kidney disease. A cautionary note: low-protein diets, if not carefully managed, can lead to malnutrition. Be sure to consult your veterinarian before making any such dietary changes.

Additional dietary options for slowing the progression of CKF may be in the offing. Dr. Freeman is optimistic about fish oils, which contain certain fatty acids that recent research suggests may reduce kidney inflammation.

Because the polyuria associated with CKF can result in the "washing out" of important water-soluble vitamins, some dogs with CKF benefit from multivitamin supplements. But since many "kind to kidney" diets already contain extra vitamins, don't add supplements without veterinary guidance.

Above all, keep a watchful eye. Report any changes in your dog's eating, drinking, and elimination habits to your veterinarian. Such changes may alert your veterinarian to the possibility of kidney disease—or allow him or her to adjust treatment if therapy has already begun. ■

4

Lyme Disease

Avoidance and control are your best bets in the fight against Lyme disease, which often defies diagnosis and treatment.

If you've ever found a tick on your dog, you know these eight-legged creatures can be fairly easy to spot. After they've hatched, ticks need a blood meal to advance from larvae to nymphs to adults. While ticks are feeding on your dog, they become large enough to see fairly easily with the naked eye. Once engorged, the tick eventually will fall from the dog's body, but that doesn't mean the danger is over. Once the tick takes a blood meal, whether from a human or a dog, there's potential for infection with Lyme disease.

The infectious organism that causes Lyme disease is Borrelia burgdorferi, a tightly coiled bacterium (spirochete). In the United States, the principal tick transmitters of B. burgdorferi to both dogs and people are the deer tick in the Northeast and Midwest, the black-legged tick in the South (both of which are subgroups of the same species—Ixodes scapularis), and the western black-legged tick (Ixodes pacificus) in the West. These ticks are much smaller than the ticks you're used to seeing on dogs.

Lyme Disease and Dogs

Although Lyme disease causes dogs discomfort, many scientists think it's a more serious disorder in people. Laboratory studies suggest that B. burgdorferi infections in dogs often result in subclini-

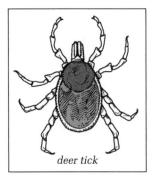

deer tick

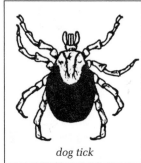

dog tick

Smaller than the average tick: The deer tick (Ixodes scapularis) is much smaller than other ticks that typically feed on dogs. Shown here is the deer tick and an adult dog tick (Dermacentor variabilis). The life cycle of the deer tick takes two years to complete. The tiny nymphs responsible for transmitting most cases of canine and human Lyme disease are most active during late spring and early summer.

cal Lyme disease (where no signs of illness occur) or self-limiting disease (where signs disappear after a few days without treatment). However, some veterinarians think natural exposure to the spirochetes is more intense than laboratory exposure, and there's some evidence, albeit scant, to suggest that infection can affect a dog's heart or kidneys.

Hot Spots

Where you and your dog live or frequently visit may dictate whether Lyme disease is a potential problem. The disease is prevalent in only a few regions, including coastal areas of Massachusetts, Connecticut, and Rhode Island; Westchester and Dutchess counties in New York; Wisconsin; Michigan's Upper Peninsula; northern Illinois; and northern California.

But even within these localities, exposure to the spirochete varies significantly. In Westchester County, New York, for example, the exposure rate in dogs ranges from 6.5 percent in densely populated municipalities to 85 percent in more sparsely populated parts of the county.

Although some veterinarians think the range of the ticks harboring B. burgdorferi is spreading, there is no hard scientific proof. It is nevertheless possible that development-driven destruction of normal deer and rodent habitats is forcing these animals (and the freeloading ticks they may carry) into closer contact with dogs and people.

What Owners Can Do

Here are ways to reduce your dog's risk of exposure to tick-borne diseases:

■ *Check your dog daily for ticks. It typically takes twelve to twenty-four hours for a feeding tick to transmit disease organisms, so prompt detection is important. Remember, though, that the ticks capable of transmitting Lyme disease are so small they may escape notice.*

■ *Put a tick collar containing amitraz on your dog. Amitraz collars kill already embedded ticks and prevent new ticks from attaching. Your dog's system does not absorb amitraz, thus the risk of adverse reactions is minimal.*

■ *Promptly remove all ticks you find. Using tweezers, grasp the tick close to the dog's skin and pull gently and steadily until the parasite lets go. Don't squeeze or burn the tick lest you propel infected tick fluids into your dog.*

■ *Mow your lawn frequently and clear leaves from your yard to create a less tick-friendly environment.*

■ *Consider having your dog vaccinated if you live in or near—or frequently visit—a Lyme-disease danger zone. But remember, no vaccine affords 100 percent protection against disease, and no vaccine is 100 percent free of side effects.*

Blood-Test Ambiguity

The main difficulty in determining the true canine prevalence of Lyme disease is the lack of ironclad diagnostic methods. The most conclusive way to diagnose bacterial infections in general is to culture the offending organisms after extracting them from the affected tissues of an ill dog. However, accomplishing this with B. burgdorferi has proven very difficult.

Blood tests that detect antibodies against B. burgdorferi can determine if a dog has been exposed to the spirochete, but currently available tests are far from 100 percent accurate. Furthermore, healthy dogs who have been vaccinated against Lyme disease will test positive for anti-Borrelia antibodies unless they receive a more specialized (and more expensive) diagnostic blood test that distinguishes antibodies stimulated by vaccination from those stimulated by natural infection. And a significant proportion of unvaccinated dogs have positive antibody tests but show no signs of illness. (These dogs have been exposed but are not technically infected.) "By itself, a positive antibody test does not mean that a dog has Lyme disease," says Dr. Linda Ross, associate professor and internist at Tufts University School of Veterinary Medicine.

Diagnosis Meets Treatment

If your dog's entire clinical picture leads your veterinarian to suspect Lyme disease, he or she may prescribe an antibiotic to treat the signs—and help confirm the diagnosis. "If the signs disappear after a few days on antibiotics, a Lyme-disease diagnosis becomes more believable," says Dr. Susan Cotter, a Tufts professor. However, the antibiotics used to treat suspected cases of Lyme disease (tetracycline or doxycycline) have inherent anti-inflammatory properties and kill off other harmful bacteria, so clinical improvement does not necessarily mean the dog had Lyme disease.

With so many questions about Lyme disease unanswered, your best bet is to practice prudent tick avoidance, control, and removal tactics. ■

5

Viral Infections

Parvovirus, distemper, and rabies all are
on the decline, thanks to increased public
awareness and scientific advances.

N ot so long ago, viral disease in dogs was common in the
United States. But today, thanks to responsible vaccination habits on the part of owners and the effectiveness of
vaccines themselves, most dogs are well protected against
these ailments.

Canine distemper and parvovirus incapacitated and killed thousands of dogs before effective vaccines became available. "Now, if
we see one case of parvo every four months, that's a lot," says Dr.
Gail Mason, a veterinarian in Brunswick, Maine. And while rabies
(a lethal viral disease that can be transmitted from dogs to people)
continues to decimate some wild-animal populations, it rarely af-
flicts dogs in the United States today.

Profiles of the Perpetrators

Despite recent success in reducing viral outbreaks, owners must still
be constantly vigilant to ensure their dog's continued good health.
The viral diseases of most concern to owners and veterinarians today
are rabies, distemper, parainfluenza, infectious hepatitis (acute liver
inflammation caused by a canine adenovirus), and the gastrointestinal ailments resulting from parvovirus and coronavirus.

For all the harm they can inflict, viruses are extremely tiny infectious agents: a stack of thirty thousand would measure less than one millimeter high. All viruses consist of a core of genetic material and an outer coat of protein. Some viruses, such as the distemper virus, have an additional outer envelope made of fats and carbohydrates. Enveloped viruses are easier to destroy because they are susceptible to sunlight, drying, and conventional disinfectants. Nonenveloped viruses like parvovirus and adenovirus, on the other hand, are highly resistant and can survive for weeks or months in the environment.

❝ DESPITE RECENT SUCCESS IN REDUCING VIRAL OUTBREAKS, OWNERS MUST STILL BE CONSTANTLY VIGILANT TO ENSURE THEIR DOG'S CONTINUED GOOD HEALTH. ❞

The Virus Life Cycle

Unlike bacteria, viruses cannot reproduce on their own. They must penetrate living host cells to make new virus particles (replicate). Although some viruses do not cause obvious damage to their host cells, other viruses commandeer the host cell's internal machinery and replicate until the host's biological resources are exhausted and the cell dies. The new viral particles then invade other cells and repeat the process.

The virus life cycle is perpetuated when an infected animal sheds new virus particles in its saliva (rabies), nasal or ocular discharges (distemper), exhaled respiratory droplets (parainfluenza), urine (adenovirus), or feces (parvovirus and coronavirus). Viruses are usually transmitted through inhalation or ingestion, but rabies transmission almost always requires a bite or saliva-laden scratch from an infected animal.

The signs of viral disease are manifested in the specific cells the viruses invade and destroy. Rabies and distemper attack the brain and spinal cord. Rabies can cause behavior changes, loss of coordination, and paralysis; distemper can cause seizures and blindness in addition to respiratory distress, vomiting, and diarrhea. The canine parainfluenza virus attacks the cells lining the upper airways and is a major contributor to kennel cough. Parvovirus and coronavirus assault the gastrointestinal tract, which results in severe vomiting and diarrhea. Canine adenovirus strikes the kidneys and liver and causes bleeding and liver failure.

Identifying the Invaders

In unvaccinated dogs, telltale clinical signs may be enough to tip off your veterinarian and lead to a diagnosis. However, veterinarians may have to employ diagnostic tests to detect viral diseases in dogs who have already been vaccinated against these diseases. "While vaccine failures don't happen often, no vaccine is 100 percent effective," notes Dr. Mason. To properly treat an ailing animal, veterinarians need to rule out other causes such as bacterial or parasitic diseases or poisons that can produce signs similar to the viral disease in question.

To help diagnose viral infections, veterinarians sometimes test tissue or fecal samples for viral antigens. Antigens are substances that stimulate the body to produce antibodies, which target and destroy disease-causing organisms. Parvovirus is the only viral disease for which in-clinic viral-antigen tests are available, so veterinary diagnostic laboratories perform most such tests.

The minute size of viruses allows them to escape detection by ordinary microscopes, so veterinary diagnostic laboratories sometimes add special antibodies tagged with fluorescent dye to tissue samples (immunofluorescence). This process "illuminates" some viruses that would otherwise be microscopically invisible. Also, if viruses are present in high enough concentrations, the enormous magnifying power of electron microscopes can detect the viruses—although electron microscopy is time- and cost-intensive and the equipment is not widely available.

Two-Pronged Defense

Without drugs to treat canine viral diseases, veterinarians stress the importance of prevention, that is, vaccinating your dog and avoiding exposure. Before bringing home a new puppy or adult dog, check out the animal's vaccination history and overall health and that of the dogs with whom he or she has been associating. Even if all are fully vaccinated and healthy, still consider isolating your new canine companion from other dogs for a couple of weeks. That way, you can be sure the animal is not incubating a viral disease and minimize the new pet's exposure to viruses that other dogs may be harboring.

Most veterinarians recommend puppies be vaccinated at six, nine, twelve, and sixteen weeks of age. (Veterinarians may use slightly different schedules according to the prevalence of certain viral diseases in their locality.) This initial vaccination series is critically important to stimulate a pup's immune system as the antibodies ingested from the mother's milk wane. Maternal antibodies, which interfere with a vaccine's ability to induce immunity, usually disappear at around eight to eleven weeks of age; so, to play it safe, veterinarians give a series of "puppy shots" at different intervals to ensure that whenever a pup meets viruses on the street, the animal's immune system will be ready and able to ward off would-be invaders. It's also important to make sure adult dogs get their booster shots on the schedule your veterinarian recommends.

Antiviral Drugs

Antiviral medications are harder to develop than antibacterial drugs (antibiotics). This is because viruses hide inside host cells, and it's difficult to develop a drug that selectively knocks out the harmful snippets of viral material without harming the healthy host cells.

Viruses do, however, have an Achilles' heel. If a drug can block replication at a specific point in the replication process, a virus cannot make copies of itself. This is the principle behind interferons (antiviral agents produced naturally by host cells).

Physicians now use synthetic interferons to treat chronic hepatitis B and C infections in people. Unfortunately, the high cost of synthetic interferon and other antiviral therapies usually limits their use to human medicine.

"No currently available antivirals have been well-studied for clinical use in dogs," says Dr. Craig Greene, professor at the University of Georgia College of Veterinary Medicine and a recognized authority on canine infectious diseases. Thus, for dogs, the best strategy is still to prevent viral infections through timely vaccination and by avoiding exposure.

Be careful about exposing your dog to other canines unless you know all the animals' parvo vaccine status.

Threat of Parvo

Imagine a lethal virus that attacks the canine community and against which dogs have no defense. Without natural immunity, infected dogs inevitably perish. Meanwhile, veterinarians work feverishly to develop a vaccine, which is a weakened form of the virus that "artificially" stimulates antibody production to fight off the virus. So it was in the late 1970s, when parvovirus first rocked the dog world.

But now, "the incidence of parvo has dropped dramatically because owners routinely vaccinate their dogs," notes Dr. Susan Cotter, professor at Tufts University School of Veterinary Medicine. Most puppies acquire temporary parvo-destroying antibodies by ingesting them through their mom's first milk (colostrum). Dogs can also develop more permanent immunity by successfully thwarting a parvo infection. And most dogs who do contract parvo nowadays survive because veterinarians diagnose the disease quickly and treat it effectively.

Detective Work

But complacency is unwise because parvo can still be lethal. While most adult dogs are immune to parvo, puppies between six weeks and six months of age are dangerously susceptible. Diagnosing a full-blown case of parvo is straightforward. If a puppy less than six months old shows up at the veterinary clinic feverish and dehydrated from vomiting and diarrhea, and if a complete blood count (CBC) test reveals low white blood cell levels, parvo is the probable culprit. Under these circumstances, the veterinarian will immediately begin treating the pup.

To conclusively diagnose parvo, the veterinarian must find evidence of the canine parvovirus strain (CPV-2) in the patient's stool. While veterinarians have access to several fairly reliable CPV-2 detection tests, these tests are not infallible. The most common problem is a false-positive reading that may show up in recently vaccinated dogs.

Viral Vigor

Like all viruses, parvovirus is a snippet of genetic material that uses the host's cellular machinery to churn out replicas of itself. (Some scientists think parvovirus is a mutation of the panleukopenia virus that affects cats.) Over a two-week period, an infected dog can shed up to a billion CPV-2 viruses in his or her feces, and they can survive in the environment for five months or longer.

When an unprotected dog ingests the virus, CPV-2 begins multiplying in the lymph tissue of the animal's nose and throat and then travels to the bone marrow, suppressing production of infection-fighting white blood cells. Hitching a ride in the bloodstream, the virus travels to the cells lining the small intestine. There, CPV-2 damages the intestinal villi, the threadlike projections that absorb fluids and nutrients. The resulting vomiting and diarrhea can lead to dehydration and dangerous imbalances in electrolytes—electrically charged chemicals essential to normal cell function.

To make matters worse, the compromised intestines lose their ability to "hem in" resident digestive bacteria, which then begin to infiltrate the bloodstream and cause systemwide infection. "Bacteria in the bloodstream of a dog with depleted white blood cells is a life-threatening combination," notes Dr. Mary Labato, clinical associate professor at Tufts University School of Veterinary Medicine.

Breeds At Risk

Certain breeds seem more prone to parvovirus, but scientists don't know why. Rottweilers and Doberman Pinschers have led the "parvo predisposed" list for several years, and recent findings suggest that pit-bull-type terriers and German Shepherds should also be included.

But crowded living conditions (like those found in "puppy mills") and concurrent disease (especially intestinal abnormalities) also increase the risk of parvo. And sexually mature, intact dogs may face a greater risk of parvo than their neutered counterparts because unneutered dogs tend to roam, increasing their exposure to infection.

Alarm Signals

The signs of parvovirus are not specific. Be on the lookout for lethargy and loss of appetite, progressing within a day or two to vomiting, diarrhea (often profuse and bloody), and high fever.

Don't wait for the more severe signs to develop. If your normally energetic dog who enjoys mealtime suddenly becomes listless and disinterested in food, play it safe and visit your veterinarian.

There is no surefire parvo preventive, but the following precautions—especially important for puppies—will increase your dog's chances of living parvo-free:

■ *Stick religiously to your dog's vaccination schedule.*

■ *Keep your pet away from dogs with unknown parvo-vaccination status.*

■ *Prevent your dog from coming in contact with feces.*

■ *Observe good hygiene at home, and if you board your dog, insist that his or her kennels and runs be disinfected daily. A 1-to-30 ratio of chlorine bleach to water is most effective against parvovirus.*

Supporting Parvo Patients

While veterinarians can't kill CPV-2, they can provide life-saving support by restoring fluid and electrolyte balance, battling systemic infection, and minimizing further fluid loss. Veterinarians typically withhold food for twelve to twenty-four hours to rest the patient's beleaguered intestinal tract while they administer electrolyte-laden fluids—either intravenously (into a vein) or subcutaneously (under the skin). The practitioner may add glucose to the recipe if the animal has low blood sugar along with infection-fighting antibiotics, antivomiting medication if vomiting is relentless, and blood transfusions if the animal is anemic.

Protection from Parvo

Immunity via vaccination is your dog's best defense against parvo. Have your dog vaccinated with a vaccine made from modified live virus—a biologically altered and harmless version of CPV-2.

Immunizing puppies presents special challenges. Although puppies born to immunized mothers are protected for a period of time, "during the first four to twelve weeks of a pup's life, maternal antibodies decline to a level where they no longer protect the puppy," notes veterinary virologist Dr. Roy Pollock, who currently is president of the consultancy Fort Hill Company in Montchanin, Delaware. But pups can't produce antibodies in response to "puppy shots" until maternal antibodies drop below protective levels. This creates a "window of susceptibility" during which maternal-antibody levels are high enough to neutralize the vaccine but too low to protect against infection. Recent improvements in parvo vaccines, however, have helped close the window of susceptibility. Veterinarians usually administer these new parvo vaccines to pups as a three-shot series, typically beginning at six to eight weeks of age, compared to the traditional four- or five-shot regimen administered to older puppies.

But no vaccine can guarantee 100 percent protection. So owners—especially "puppy parents"—must be vigilant about their animal's comings and goings. Keep your pup away from other dogs with uncertain vaccination status—and from areas where such dogs congregate. Before enrolling your pet in puppy kindergarten, make sure the instructor requires proof of vaccination for all participants.

But even taking every known precaution, you can't completely eliminate the risk of CPV-2 infection.

About SARS

Back in late 2002 through mid 2003, a Severe Acute Respiratory Syndrome (SARS) outbreak caused nearly 800 deaths worldwide. The cause was a coronavirus mutation that had likely jumped the species barrier between animal and humans. Chinese police, in an effort to block the spread of the disease, began killing dogs despite a lack of scientific data and the advice of veterinarians.

"Coronavirus is not a big entity in dogs," says Dr. Elizabeth Rozanski, assistant professor of emergency and critical care at Tufts University School of Veterinary Medicine. "It's basically vomiting and diarrhea, relegated to the bottom of infectious diseases in veterinary medicine."

Although not considered a serious health problem, canine coronavirus (CCV) may be the second most frequent cause of enteritis—infectious inflammation of part of the intestinal tract—in dogs. Some evidence indicates that natural CCV infection without illness occasionally occurs in dogs. One study found that 61 percent of dogs with diarrhea were positive for corona, while 45 percent of healthy dogs had antibodies to the virus but had never shown signs of the disease. Prevalence of the naturally occurring disease varies as much as zero to 80 percent.

Usually, healthy adult dogs don't get sick if exposed to corona, but puppies or debilitated dogs are more prone to infection. Symptoms appear quickly and can start with an episode of vomiting. Fever isn't always present but is possible.

Diarrhea quickly follows with a foul odor and an orange or greenish-yellow color. Sick dogs can also experience mild weakness, lethargy, and loss of appetite. The illness tends to be self-limiting, lasting only a few days. Because of the amount of fluid lost through diarrhea, puppies can dehydrate quickly. Although death due to coronavirus is uncommon, dehydration is the cause when it does occur.

While the American Animal Hospital Association Vaccine Study Task Force has recommended against corona vaccination, some veterinarians support using the vaccine. Many preparations routinely include the vaccine for corona as part of a multidisease single-shot vaccination. If your dog is receiving a vaccine against distemper, hepatitis, and others, chances are about 50 percent he or she will also be vaccinated against corona.

Supporting Sick Dogs

Few if any antiviral medications are available for fighting viral infections in dogs. When dogs contract viral diseases, veterinarians usually provide only supportive therapy until the infection runs its course. Supportive therapy may include keeping a canine patient clean and warm; using antibiotics if a secondary bacterial infection develops; and administering intravenous fluids to replace water and nutrients lost through vomiting and diarrhea. ■

6

Gastrointestinal Problems

Dogs diagnosed with problems such as inflammatory bowel syndrome and ulcers can have excellent quality of life with the proper treatment.

Millions of Americans have gastrointestinal problems of one sort or another, from inflammatory bowel disease to ulcers. What you may not know is that GI problems also can strike your dog. The forms of diagnosis and the treatments can vary.

This chapter provides information about three disorders: IBD, ulcers, and a problem called megaesophagus, or an enlarged esophagus. Please keep in mind that because GI problems frequently involve vomiting and diarrhea, they may result in dangerous dehydration. We encourage you to consult your veterinarian promptly when such problems occur.

Inflammatory Bowel Disease (IBD)

IBD is a group of disorders that result in chronic stimulation of inflammation in the gastrointestinal tract. The inflammation causes frequent, recurring episodes of vomiting and/or diarrhea. But diagnosing and treating the condition can be difficult.

Some researchers believe IBD is an autoimmune response where the body either overreacts to a foreign antigen—a substance that provokes an immune response—or reacts inappropriately to a normal antigen, such as a food protein.

Possible precipitators can be a bacterial, viral or protozoal infection; parasitic infestation; hypersensitivity or intolerance to dietary ingredients; digestive enzyme deficiencies; or intestinal wall defects.

"No one really knows what the most frequent or likely triggers are," says Mary Labato, clinical associate professor of internal medicine at Tufts University School of Veterinary Medicine. "There is no single, overwhelming type or cause."

Symptoms and Diagnosis

Because IBD can affect different portions of the GI tract, symptoms vary greatly. Besides diarrhea or vomiting, other signs may include gurgling stomach; belching; gas, loss of appetite; desperation to get outside to eliminate; soiling in the house; pain with bowel movements; weight loss; and blood in the stool.

Veterinarians do blood work to rule out other problems, such as pancreatitis, Addison's and kidney disease or malignancy. They examine fecal samples for worms or infections such as giardia. They also may take X-rays and use ultrasound to check for obstructions or other abnormalities. A diagnostic test for IBD is a positive biopsy, obtained through an endoscopy of the stomach or a colonoscopy of the lower GI tract. But results still may be unclear.

"Even among pathologists, there's a great deal of difference in scoring the amount of white blood cells found in the intestinal lining to say, 'This is IBD,'" Dr. Labato says. "One may read test findings as abnormal, or another one will describe the inflammation as mild or a slight increase but normal."

Treatment

The treatment goals in IBD are to eliminate an identifiable cause, reduce diarrhea and vomiting, decrease bowel inflammation and stabilize the dog's weight. After gaining control over acute episodes, long-term management may come down to diet.

If food sensitivity is a contributing factor, it's likely the ingredient has been in the diet for many months. All foods used in the past or being currently fed, including treats, are eliminated.

Then a "novel protein," a source never eaten previously and one that is easy to digest, is substituted. Rabbit, duck, venison and kangaroo are common sources. Fats are moderately restricted because they lengthen the time it takes to digest food, increasing the likeli-

Shar-Peis are among the dogs in which IBD is most frequently diagnosed.

hood of nausea. Special products that meet these requirements are available from a variety of commercial manufacturers and veterinarians offering prescription IBD diets.

Veterinarians may suggest a bland diet while getting vomiting or diarrhea under control. Dr. Labato recommends a mixture of cottage cheese and rice for her patients. Other options are boiled hamburger and rice or chicken and rice, along with short-term use of Kaopectate or Pepto-Bismol, anti-diarrheal liquids.

"If it's true IBD, you treat it a little differently," says Dr. Matthew Krecic, a small animal internal medicine specialist who is a consultant with IDEXX Telemedicine, a service for veterinarians. "Food sensitivity may respond with diet alone, but you may have to manage IBD with other medications" as well.

Because it can take two to six weeks for improvement, dogs who are showing worse symptoms or who have lost too much weight will likely take other medications simultaneously.

Drugs also can be part of the treatment. "Which drugs are best depends on the severity of signs, how recurrent they are and the animal's overall condition," Dr. Labato says. "I'm inclined to use Flagyl (an anti-protozoal antibiotic also known as metronidazole) and steroids (corticosteroids, cortisone, prednisone, Prednisolone, etc.), or a combination of drugs based on the symptomology."

Additional categories of drugs that may help include: compounds containing a sulfa anti-biotic, antiinflammatory and mild immunosuppressants (sulfasalzine, mesalamine); other antibiotics such as Tylan or tetracycline; other immunosuppressants to suppress an over-reactive immune system (azathioprine, chlorambucil); anti-spasmodics or anti-hypermotility agents that relieve abdominal cramping or slow the digestive tract; or prescription-strength acid inhibitors like Pepcid, Prilosec, or Prevacid.

Breeds Likely To Develop IBD

Researchers don't always agree on the breeds prone to developing IBD, but these seem to be diagnosed with the condition more than others:

Basenji, Boxer, Cocker Spaniel, Dalmatian, German Shepherd, Irish Setter, Lundehund, Shar-Pei, Rottweiler, Soft-coated Wheaten Terrier and Yorkshire Terrier.

The types of IBD they develop are sometimes considered variants of the more common form of the condition, with different types of inflammatory cells attacking different gastrointestinal tissue. Treatment is nearly identical but depends on the type of cells affected, location of the inflammation and the dog's symptoms.

Although a dog can have IBD at any age, the average age at diagnosis is about six years. The disease affects males and females equally.

Ulcers

An ulcer is a damaged area on the surface of any mucous membrane that doesn't heal. It spreads through a process called ulceration, involving the death of minute portions of healthy tissues around its edges. Dogs usually develop multiple ulcers, although in some cases a single, large ulcer may be associated with a tumor. The prevalence of gastrointestinal ulcers in dogs is low compared to that in people.

Ulcers typically occur in the stomach, where they're known as gastric ulcers, or in the first few centimeters of the small intestine in the duodenum, where they're called duodenal ulcers. They range in diameter from several millimeters to four centimeters, or about an inch and a half. A layer of mucus protects the mucosa, the inner protective lining of the stomach and duodenum from the corrosive and digestive effects of gastric acid and the enzyme pepsin.

Dogs seem particularly prone to gastric erosion and ulceration related to NSAIDs (non-steroidal anti-inflammatory drugs such as aspirin). These weak acids that concentrate and cause damage when they penetrate the epithelial, or protective, cells lining the gastrointestinal tract. They inhibit prostaglandin production, which leads to reduced blood flow, decreased mucous and bicarbonate secretion, reduced epithelial cell turnover and the breakdown of mucosal defense mechanisms. Aspirin and phenylbutazone were the first NSAIDs to be widely used in dogs.

The ulcer-inducing properties of corticosteroids, including prednisone, Prednisolone and Dexamethasone, most often apply when they're used for a long period of time. Dogs with spinal cord lesions undergoing surgery and receiving corticosteroids are prone to hemorrhagic gastroenteritis and perforating colonic ulcers. Ulcers in the duodenum can occur with liver failure. Gastrin-producing pancreatic tumors and pancreatic polypeptide-producing pancreatic tumors also have been associated with gastric or duodenal ulceration in dogs.

Symptoms and Diagnosis

Dogs with gastric ulceration may not display any symptoms, or they may intermittently vomit fresh, red blood or digested blood, resembling coffee grounds.

Other symptoms can include diarrhea, abdominal pain and dark, tarry feces. In long-term cases, the dogs may lose weight and have poor body condition. If severe gastrointestinal hemorrhage has occurred, weakness and pale mucous membranes or circulatory shock may be present. The worst scenario for ulcer disease is perforation of the stomach or duodenum and subsequent peritonitis. Although uncommon, it may occur with minimal warning.

Ultrasonography and contrast X-rays offer noninvasive diagnostic techniques for evaluating dogs with gastritis or ulceration. Whereas X-rays show the size and shape of the organs, ultrasound provides a view of the internal structures. With abdominal ultrasound, no anesthesia or sedation is needed if the patient is cooperative. However, if biopsies are to be taken, a short-acting anesthetic will be used.

With contrast X-rays, patients are administered barium sulfate, which coats the walls of the gastrointestinal tract. A series of X-rays are taken over several hours as it passes through. If results are negative and an ulcer is still suspected, endoscopy should be considered. It requires general anesthesia but is superior to X-rays for detecting esophageal ulcers and ulcers on the stomach wall. During an endoscopic exam, veterinarians use a thin flexible scope with a fiber-optic light source to view internal organs.

Treatment

Various drug treatments are available. "Drug treatment includes the use of a histamine-blocker; proton pump inhibitors, such as Omeprazole (Losec), in dogs with severe ulceration; and surface-coating agents if the history strongly suggests ulceration due to NSAIDs, stress and/or a mast cell tumor," Dr. Labato says. Histamine-blocking drugs include cimetidine (Tagamet) and ranitidine (Zantac). Proton pump inhibitors markedly decrease the production of stomach acid.

The newest drug, misoprostol (Cytotec), is a synthetic prostaglandin that prevents or heals ulcers associated with NSAIDs. It's more effective than sucralfate or histamine-blocking agents in preventing ulcers or erosions in dogs with arthritis who require long-term NSAID therapy.

If the patient hasn't improved with medication or severe bleeding occurs, surgical removal of the ulcer may be necessary. The pancreas can also be carefully evaluated for possible tumors.

In dogs with acute gastric disorders, treatment frequently begins with the withholding of food and water for one or two days. Once the dog can tolerate small amounts of water or ice every few hours, he or she is given small amounts of food six to eight times daily. If no vomiting occurs, the amount is increased over three to four days and the number of feedings is decreased to two or three meals daily. If the dog vomits during this period, food is withdrawn and offered after a few hours.

The other feeding method uses food and nutrients to stimulate secretions that re-establish normal bowel motility and function. Dogs are fed bland diets in frequent, small amounts. Veterinarians recommend a low-fat liquid diet, low in non-digestible fiber with highly digestible carbohydrates as the main source of calories to reduce gastric acid secretion.

Reducing protein in the very short term may help dogs with gastritis and ulceration because it reduces acid secretion.

Ultimately, the prognosis depends on the underlying cause, size, and depth of the ulcer, and complications, such as severe hemorrhage, perforation or peritonitis. The prognosis is poor for dogs with ulcers associated with chronic kidney or liver disease.

For dogs with malignant gastric tumors that are most commonly diagnosed in an advanced state, the survival time is six months or less, even with surgical intervention. The prognosis is good for dogs with peptic ulcers and benign gastric tumors if the initiating conditions can be successfully treated.

Ulcer Terms

- **Gastrin:** *A hormone, secreted by the mucous lining of the stomach, which stimulates the secretion of gastric acid.*

- **Gastrinomas:** *Tumors, produced by the pancreas, that secrete the hormone gastrin, which in turn stimulates production of gastric juices that cause ulcers. Gastrinomas may be malignant or benign.*

- **Gastritis:** *Inflammation of the stomach lining that may or may not indicate an ulcer or cancer.*

- **Laparotomy:** *The surgical opening of the abdominal cavity.*

- **Mast cell tumors:** *Also known as mastocytomas, occur in the intestines and liver and produce histamine.*

- **Peptic ulcer:** *An ulcer in the lower end of the esophagus, stomach or duodenum caused by secretion of pepsin, an enzyme produced in the mucosal lining of the stomach.*

- **Peritonitis:** *Inflammation of the peritoneum, the membrane that lines the abdominal wall and covers the abdominal organs.*

- **Prostaglandins:** *Potent hormone-like substances that control muscle contractions and inflammation. NSAIDs reduce prostaglandin synthesis by inhibiting cyclooxygenase.*

Enlarged Esophagus

The esophagus connects the throat to the stomach and, when food enters the esophagus, peristalsis—a neurological reflex causing muscles to contract and relax—begins moving food to the stomach. Megaesophagus is a condition in which the esophagus becomes enlarged or dilated. It results in regurgitation and may cause failure to thrive and aspiration pneumonia.

Owners can easily confuse regurgitation with vomiting. Regurgitation is passive. Swallowed food sits in the esophagus until it simply falls out minutes or hours later. Vomiting is active, accompanied by gagging, heaving and retching as the body expels stomach contents. "Megaesophagus is the most common cause of regurgitation in dogs," says Dr. Labato. "It may be a primary disorder or secondary to esophageal obstruction or neuromuscular dysfunction."

Among the causes: neuromuscular diseases, including myasthenia gravis, polymyositis (a muscle disease), polyneuropathy (affecting the peripheral nerves), dysautonomia (a rare disease involving the autonomic nervous system), systemic lupus erythematosus (an immune-mediated disease), polyradiculoneuritis (inflammation of the peripheral nerves and spinal ganglia), central nervous system disease, botulism and damage to the bilateral vagal nerve, which carries messages to and from the brain.

Congenital megaesophagus occurs in young dogs and is a developmental abnormality of the esophagus. More frequently, larger dogs are diagnosed with the idiopathic form in which the cause is unknown. Adult onset megaesophagus occurs spontaneously in dogs seven to fifteen years of age. Susceptible breeds include Irish Setters, German Shepherds, Golden Retrievers, Shar-Peis, Great Danes, Miniature Schnauzers, Wirehair Fox Terriers, Newfoundlands, Pugs, and Greyhounds.

Some dogs appear to outgrow the disorder, while others show no improvement and owners must continually manage their feeding. Dogs with secondary megaesophagus, as with myasthenia gravis, may go into remission and improve with appropriate treatment.

"In most cases we don't know the cause," says Dr. David C. Twedt, a faculty member at the College of Veterinary Medicine and Biomedical Sciences at Colorado State University in Fort Collins. "Twenty-five percent of the cases have an underlying cause with the most common being myasthenia gravis."

Symptoms and Diagnosis

Clinical signs of megaesophagus are regurgitation, wasting and malnutrition, halitosis, hypersalivation, bulging esophagus at the neck, cough and increased respiratory effort due to pneumonia and muscle weakness, Dr. Labato says.

To confirm a diagnosis, veterinarians usually take X-rays. Other tests, which are intended to identify the underlying cause, may include a complete blood count, chemistry profile, urinalysis,

ACTH (adrenocorticotropic hormone) stimulation test, thyroid function test, an acetylcholine receptor antibody titer to diagnose myasthenia gravis and an antinuclear antibody titer, which is a blood test that looks for immune-mediated disease in which the body attacks itself.

In a review of cases of dogs with megaesophagus with no identifiable cause, owners euthanized 65 percent of them within a three-month period, Dr. Twedt says. "The prognosis is better if the etiology [cause] is identified and can be treated."

Treatment

Veterinarians can diagnose the problem, but in the end dog owners have to deal with a dog with special needs. "These cases may be very difficult to handle, and it takes a very dedicated owner to manage and treat a pet with megaesophagus," Dr. Labato says.

Veterinarians advise owners to feed their dogs in an upright position—an elevated dog bowl works well—so gravity will help move food to the stomach. Dr. Twedt suggests owners offer several types of food to find the ones best suited to their dog—from gruel to meatballs and everything in between. "Hand feeding canned food made into individual 'meatballs' seems to be well tolerated in many cases with less of a problem of aspiration," he says.

Malnutrition can become a significant problem. In extreme cases, veterinarians recommend a feeding tube.

Consult Your Veterinarian

Any time your dog is exhibiting diarrhea or vomiting/regurgitation beyond his or her normal behavior, it's time to see your veterinarian. Dogs can easily become dehydrated, exacerbating what may already be a dangerous medical situation. Your veterinarian will be able to help determine what's behind the symptoms. ■

7

Diabetes

*With proper regulation of insulin,
diet, and exercise, a diabetic dog can
have a normal lifespan.*

When a veterinarian tells clients their dog has diabetes
mellitus, they're understandably upset. Their reaction
is usually based on fear of the unknown, worry about
their dog's early demise, and misunderstanding of the
treatment for this metabolic disease. And it is true that diabetic dogs
may encounter complications, such as blindness from cataracts and
potentially fatal hypoglycemic events.

However, once the pet's insulin is regulated and the dog has a
consistent routine, managing the disease generally is easier than
owners expect. Given proper treatment, a diabetic dog should have
a normal lifespan, says Michael Stone, assistant clinical professor
at Tufts University School of Veterinary Medicine.

Humans have either Type 1 diabetes, which is lack of insulin, or
Type 2, which means that the pancreas produces insulin but the
cells in the body are resistant to it. Dogs have Type 1. No one knows
why, but it occurs twice as often in female dogs as in males; onset
usually occurs around the age of nine.

Causes and Symptoms

The most common cause of diabetes in dogs is probably an autoimmune problem within the pancreas. Obesity and heredity are
risk factors. Inflammations of the pancreas, as occurs with pancre-

atitis, and hormonal diseases like Cushing's can predispose dogs to diabetes. Sometimes, pregnancy and the reproductive cycle of unspayed females create insulin resistance that can cause either temporary or permanent diabetes.

The lack of insulin sets up a complex series of occurrences that results in diabetes. The body's cells use a kind of sugar called glucose as food, but the cells can't use the glucose without enough of the hormone insulin. Insulin helps a dog use or store the glucose received from food. When there isn't enough insulin, the glucose isn't available as an energy source. Weight loss occurs because the body goes into a starvation mode even though adequate glucose remains in the blood. The cells can't access the glucose, and the extra glucose goes into the urine.

Diabetes' most common signs are increased water consumption and urination. Others are increased appetite, weight loss and weakness. Veterinarians base their diagnosis on clinical signs, physical examination and lab tests; the tests typically show hyperglycemia (elevated blood sugar) and glucose in the urine. In severe cases, waste products called ketones are in the urine or blood. Normal bodies rid themselves of ketones, but diabetic dogs can't eliminate them quickly enough to prevent a buildup in the blood. The increased quantity is toxic.

A Diabetes Primer

While diabetes mellitus is by far the most common form of diabetes in dogs, it's not the only kind. Diabetes insipidus, a very rare disease unrelated to diabetes mellitus, involves a deficiency in the vasopressin antidiuretic hormones. It results from a lack of production from the pituitary gland in the brain.

"Diabetes mellitus and diabetes insipidus have their origin in ancient times. In Latin, diabetes means 'run through' as in too much urine," says Tufts' Dr. Stone.

"Mellitus means 'sweet.' Insipidus means 'tasteless.' Tasting the urine was how the diseases were diagnosed before modern testing was available. The sugar made the urine from patients with diabetes mellitus sweet." Secondary diabetes is diagnosed when treatment of a primary disease allows the diabetes to resolve.

For example, if pancreatitis resolves, then hormone production of insulin may return. Secondary diabetes is rare in dogs. Generally, healthy dogs won't develop secondary diabetes.

"We do sometimes see 'pre-diabetics' that will develop a disease and become temporarily diabetic, then the diabetes will resolve after treatment of the primary disease," says Dr. Stone. "However, these patients will go on to develop diabetes within a few months without an underlying cause.

"Will it eventually resolve? Rarely. Occasionally, an unspayed female dog will develop diabetes after being in heat and the diabetes will permanently go into remission after ovariohysterectomy. Some patients receiving potent anti-insulin drugs, such as edroxyprogesterone acetate, will go into remission after the drug is stopped. But these are a small percentage of the total cases of diabetics. In most cases for dogs, once a diabetic, forever a diabetic."

About Your Dog's Glucose Level

A normal blood glucose level for a dog is the same as humans, about 100 milligrams/deciliter of blood (mg/dl). High sugar generally isn't an emergency except in extreme cases, such as greater than 800 mg/dl, Dr. Stone says. Blood glucose levels can be altered by several factors, including eating, exercise, and stress. It's important the level remains as close to normal as possible.

Dogs can be given a glucose curve test on a regular basis to see how well the diabetes is being controlled and determine if changes should be made. The test measures blood glucose every one to two hours throughout a day. Some veterinarians recommend diabetic dogs have a glucose curve run every two to four months if all appears to be well. However, the tests have spurred controversy.

"New information suggests that blood sugar curves, as performed by veterinarians, are fraught with error," Dr. Stone says. "In a recent study, blood sugar curves were generated on two consecutive days on the same patient receiving the same dose of insulin. The results were so different between Day One and Day Two that different recommendations would have been made 60 percent of the time. I used to recommend frequent blood sugar curves. I now rely more upon the patient's clinical signs—whether they are drinking excessively or not—and results of urine glucose tests the owners tell me over the phone. I perform fewer blood sugar curves now than I used to."

These days, owners are taught how to safely draw blood from their pets, allowing them to check blood sugars at home. If performed properly, this information may be useful but is subject to the same problems as in-hospital sugar testing.

Basic Treatment

Diabetic dogs are treated with insulin injections, diet modifications, and exercise. Veterinarians instruct owners on insulin injection. Insulin available in the United States is human grade, so owners buy it and syringes at human pharmacies. It can be difficult to determine appropriate doses of insulin when treatment begins.

Sometimes, the owner isn't sure if the dog received the entire dose of insulin; the dog wriggles away, or insulin spills on his or her coat. "The recommendation still is to skip that dose if you're unsure it went in. It's always better to underdose than overdose," says Dr. Stone. The critical factor in treatment is consistency; the dog should have the same food at the same time every day and the same exercise.

Complications

Unfortunately, diabetes has complications. "Almost every dog—up to 90 percent—develops blindness due to cataracts," Dr. Stone says. "The cataracts may be surgically removed and complete vision returned; however, surgery is expensive and must be performed by a specialist."

Cataracts are the result of prolonged blood sugar being higher than normal. It's almost impossible to keep the blood sugar tightly regulated so that cataracts are prevented. When they develop, the dog can seem to go blind almost overnight.

"Hypoglycemia—low blood sugar causing weakness—is the most feared complication," Dr. Stone says. "If hypoglycemia does occur, it can usually be prevented in the future by reducing the dose of insulin."

Hypoglycemia can be life threatening. It develops when the dog has excessive insulin or insufficient food. Signs, which escalate as

> **INFECTION IN THE URINARY SYSTEM CAN CAUSE URINARY STRAINING, BLOOD IN THE URINE, FEVER, AND LOSS OF APPETITE.**

the degree of hypoglycemia increases, include lack of coordination, weakness, personality change, trembling, sleepiness, loss of vision, confusion, seizures and coma.

The treatment: Apply corn syrup to the gums. It's helpful if owners keep a squeeze bottle filled with corn syrup for hypoglycemic episodes. Dr. Stone recommends feeding a meal and immediately contacting your veterinarian for additional instructions. If the veterinarian is unavailable, feed a meal and withhold insulin until you receive medical advice, hopefully within twelve hours.

Urinary tract infections often accompany diabetes because bacteria like to grow in the sugary urine, Dr. Stone says. "Poor diabetic control can result in urinary accidents in the house. A diabetic dog owner should be in close contact with the veterinarian and visit at least a minimum of four times per year for testing of the urine for infection."

Some diseases can run concurrently with diabetes. "Inflammation of the pancreas (pancreatitis) should be considered when a diabetic begins vomiting," says Dr. Stone. "Infection in the urinary system can cause urinary straining, blood in the urine, fever, and loss of appetite. Internal infections in the kidney, liver, or lungs may also cause fever and loss of appetite. Low thyroid levels and altered cortisol hormone levels may also occur in diabetics."

The concurrent diseases sometimes precede and follow diabetes' onset. "In some patients one disease is seen before the other, and in other patients two or more diseases are diagnosed concurrently," says Dr. Stone. "Whether one disease predisposes to the other or whether there's a common disease affecting two or more organs is sometimes difficult to pin down. For example, diabetes may occur because of an immune system mediated destruction of the pancreatic cells. Sometimes the immune system also targets similar cells in the thyroid or adrenal gland at the same time. Dysfunction of one or more glands may occur at the same time or one first, then the other."

For More Information

- *The Web site* **www.petdiabetes.org** *provides extensive information for owners of diabetic pets, including message boards, a mailing list, suggestions on the type of blood glucose meters to buy, and a listing of diabetic dogs available for adoption.*

- *The Society for Comparative Endocrinology at* **www.compendo.org** *is a veterinary organization with an interest in diabetes. Its goal is to promote the scientific understanding of endocrine physiology to help diagnosis, treatment, and prevention of endocrine diseases, and thereby improve the quality of life of animals and people.* ■

8

Ailments of Older Dogs

Canine cognitive dysfunction and Cushing's disease are among the challenges your older dog may face.

Maybe your dog isn't quite as quick to chase a ball, or maybe he or she seems a bit more disoriented in new settings than was the case in the past. Chances are that your dog may have joined the ranks of the 18 million dogs in the United States who are seven or older.

Veterinarians generally consider small dogs to be senior citizens at about twelve years old while large dogs reach the senior stage at eight to ten years. This roughly corresponds to the fifty-five-plus category in people. Aging dogs may experience health problems that are uncommon in younger dogs, including diabetes mellitus; kidney, heart, and liver disease; hormonal anomalies such as Cushing's disease; periodontal disease; arthritis; and cancer.

To catch age-related disorders at the earliest possible stage, veterinarians often perform disease-screening blood tests during annual checkups for older dogs. A yearly examination is roughly equivalent to a person seeing a physician every five years; some veterinarians now recommend biannual visits.

Cognitive Dysfunction Syndrome (CDS)

Recent studies indicate 25 percent of dogs one to twelve years of age show some signs of cognitive impairment related to orientation in the home or yard, social interaction, housetraining or the sleep/wake cycle. The percentage of fifteen- to sixteen-year-old dogs with signs of cognitive impairment increases to almost 70 percent, says Raymond Kudej, assistant professor at Tufts University School of Veterinary Medicine.

New medications, behavior modifications, and nutrition are your best weapons to combat age-related cognitive impairment, says Dominik Faissler, clinical assistant professor of neurology at Tufts. He treats many older dogs with Anipryl (selegiline hydrochloride), a memory-improving medication manufactured by Pfizer that received Food and Drug Administration approval in late 1998. "Anipryl changes the neurotransmitters in the brain to help dogs function better and interact better with their owners," Dr. Faissler says. However, not all dogs who are given Anipryl see significant improvements.

Cushing's Disease

Middle-aged to older dogs also are more prone to Cushing's disease. Because its symptoms—constant panting, frequent urination, ravenous appetite, hair loss and muscle weakness—can mimic those of aging, it often goes undetected and untreated. Beagles, Boston Terriers, Boxers, Dachshunds, Miniature and Toy Poodles, German Shepherds, Golden Retrievers, and Yorkshire Terriers are most often affected.

Cushing's may cause serious complications—urinary tract infections, pulmonary embolisms sudden blockage of an artery by a blood clot) and blindness—but the majority of dogs with it die from the effects of old age, such as kidney or heart failure.

The disease, also know as hyperadrenocorticism, occurs when too much cortisone is in the body. This develops most

Golden Labradors are among the dogs most often affected by Cushing's disease.

commonly when the adrenal glands produce too much cortisone. The hormone cortisol is responsible for maintaining a normal blood glucose level, facilitates metabolism of fat, and supports the vascular and nervous systems. When too much is produced, it will affect all of the supporting systems of the body—the skeletal muscles, red blood cell production, immune system, and kidneys. By the time dogs exhibit signs of Cushing's that owners and veterinarians can see, they have damage to the liver, kidneys, and heart.

Excessive hormone secretion can be caused by underlying abnormal or benign tumors in the pituitary gland or from benign or malignant tumors within the adrenal glands themselves. More than 80 to 85 percent of dogs with Cushing's have the pituitary-dependent hyperadrenocorticism (PDH) form of the disease.

With the pituitary-dependent form of Cushing's, many veterinarians prescribe Lysodren (mitotane). It destroys the outer layer of the adrenal glands, which limits their ability to produce cortisol in response to signals to the hyperactive pituitary gland. Initially, there is an induction phase when the medication is given, and the dog is given Lysodren every day for seven to fourteen days. This is followed by a maintenance dose given once a week. Owners must carefully monitor the amount of food and water a dog takes as well as the animal's overall disposition. This helps them recognize when the drug is taking effect because symptoms will abate.

Veterinarians recommend the dogs have follow-up blood tests, a urinalysis and ACTH suppression tests every three to four months. The cost of identifying, treating and monitoring a dog with Cushing's can range from several hundred dollars to several thousand, depending upon the severity of the case and the number of tests required.

Some veterinarians prescribe Anipryl, which is also used to treat Parkinson's disease in people and cognitive dysfunction in dogs. It's thought Anipryl may alleviate the clinical signs of Cushing's by restoring the natural balance of important brain chemicals, especially dopamine.

Lumps

Lumps and bumps are found in a variety of places on a dog's body and are not necessarily cause for excessive concern. Lipomas, fatty tumors found under the skin, are most common in middle-aged or older dogs, and overweight female dogs are particularly prone to them. Once a dog gets one lipoma, more are likely to follow.

These soft, rounded lumps aren't painful to the dog if touched. Most often they're found underneath the skin, but they occasionally can be found deeper in the body, where they pose little threat to health.

Doberman Pinschers, Miniature Schnauzers, and Labrador Retrievers, in addition to mixed breeds, seem to have a genetic predisposition to develop lipomas.

"In dogs, probably 90 percent of skin lumps are benign," says John Berg, chair of Tufts' Department of Clinical Sciences. "They don't even need to be removed. Some dogs are genetically predisposed to bumps, and can have ten to twenty of them, all benign."

Benign growths stay in place and don't metastasize, or spread; however, they can grow to significant size, large enough that they can interfere with the dog's movement or functions.

"Owners should periodically look all over and feel all over the dog to check for lumps," Dr. Berg says. "It's amazing how large and advanced they can get in hidden places like under the armpit, and it can be difficult to treat them if they get huge. If owners find a new lump, they shouldn't ignore it. See your veterinarian. Wait and see might be the best approach, but ask your veterinarian if that is appropriate for a certain lump."

Your veterinarian may suggest that a lump be aspirated, a procedure that allows cells from the lump to be examined in a laboratory. No sedation or anesthesia is necessary as a needle is inserted into the lump and a plunger withdraws some cells through suction. It's not a painful procedure. Most dogs don't even notice that it's happening. Veterinarians examine the cells under a microscope, and the results can be had within minutes.

A needle aspirate usually will indicate if the lump is benign. The main purpose of a needle aspirate is to rule out a mast cell—a connective tissue cell—tumor.

If the lump is benign, there's no need to remove it unless it impedes the dog's comfort because of its location or threatens to become difficult to remove if it continues to grow. However, the veterinarian will instruct the owner to watch for any changes in it.

A biopsy is a more involved, accurate procedure. Tissue is collected for examination under a microscope. A biopsy requires general anesthesia or at least heavy sedation, and it takes two to four days for the results to be processed. "The biopsy is the gold standard for determining what's going on," Dr. Berg says. "Owners should not fear that a biopsy or aspirate will make a lump become or behave worse. If your veterinarian recommends it, feel comfortable going forward with it as it's a standard workup test."

It's true that your older dog is more susceptible to certain disorders and ailments than that playful pup next door. But working in tandem with your veterinarian, you can help make these years truly golden for your dog.

About Hypertension

You may be surprised to hear that dogs, like humans, can suffer from systemic hypertension, also known as high blood pressure. Hypertension can affect the cardiovascular system, kidneys, central nervous system, and even the eyes. It can create life-threatening problems if left untreated.

Simply put, the term hypertension refers to abnormal elevation of the pressure circulating blood exerts against blood vessels and organs. When the pressure becomes higher than ideal, stress and damage to those structures may result. In addition, the heart is forced to shoulder an increased workload and may suffer problems.

"High blood pressure in dogs rarely occurs as a stand-alone disorder," said Dr. Linda Ross, associate professor at Tufts University School of Veterinary Medicine. "Virtually all cases occur in dogs that have one of several diseases associated with hypertension, the most common of which are kidney failure, hyperadrenocorticism (Cushing's disease) and diabetes mellitus." (For more information about kidney failure and diabetes, see pages 49 and 85 in this book.)

Increased thirst or water intake can be a sign of one of the diseases associated with high blood pressure, such as Cushing's disease or diabetes. If your dog is drinking more than normal, take him or her for a veterinary exam.

"The best option is to treat the underlying disease," Dr. Ross says. "If that can be cured or controlled, blood pressure can return to normal." ■

Section II

Conditions

9

Respiratory Ailments

*Your dog's respiratory system helps protect
him or her against pollen and bacteria and acts
as an air-conditioning system.*

A dog's first respiratory system line of defense is in the nasal
cavity, where microscopic hairs (cilia) bathed in mucus
trap particles. If inhaled particles penetrate to the lungs,
macrophages (large cells whose name means "big eaters")
ingest the invaders.

If these defense mechanisms fail, a dog can develop respiratory
problems. The most common diseases of the upper respiratory tract
(the airways from the nose to the bronchi) are kennel cough (infectious tracheobronchitis) and chronic bronchitis.

Kennel cough is caused by highly contagious bacteria (most no-
tably Bordetella bronchiseptica) and/or viruses (such as canine
parainfluenza virus) that damage the lining of the upper airways.
Dogs with kennel cough have a dry, honking cough, often followed
by retching.

Veterinarians think canine chronic bronchitis results from chronically irritated airways or from increased sensitivity to inhaled allergens or pollutants. Dogs with chronic bronchitis have frequent
bouts of dry coughing. Small, urban dogs and those exposed to cig-
arette smoke are most often affected.

Because it is not infectious, chronic bronchitis does not respond
to antibiotics and can be difficult to treat. The best approach is to remove the inciting irritant from the dog's environment–or vice versa.

"Chronic bronchitis is incurable and fairly uncommon," says Dr.
Michael Stone, assistant clinical professor at Tufts University School

of Veterinary Medicine. "The general practitioner probably sees three or four cases a year. Kennel cough is very common but in no way predisposes to the development of chronic bronchitis. Chronic bronchitis develops for poorly understood reasons but is in most cases related to a hypersensitivity or allergic response to an inhaled allergen."

Lower Respiratory Problems

The most common disease of the lower respiratory tract is pneumonia, a potentially life-threatening lung ailment arising from infection with various bacteria, viruses, or fungi. Dogs with pneumonia experience an increased respiratory rate and difficulty breathing, and they may run fevers of 103 to 106 degrees Fahrenheit.

Veterinarians who suspect pneumonia may take a complete blood count to check for increased numbers of white blood cells, an indicator of infection. They may also take lung X-rays (radiographs) to determine the extent of infection. Practitioners also may infuse saline solution into the trachea and then remove it so they can microscopically examine it to identify the causative microorganism. Veterinarians treat bacterial and fungal infections with drugs, but viral pneumonia can only be treated symptomatically. Intensive care with intravenous fluids and medications such as bronchodilators (drugs that widen the airways) is sometimes necessary in severe cases. Cancer, caused by the infiltration of abnormally replicating cells, can also impair lung function.

Your Dog's Air Conditioner

The respiratory system is also your dog's main air-conditioning system. Cooling occurs via evaporation as air passes over the saliva-laden mucous membranes of the tongue and throat. As things heat up, your dog's tongue hangs out to allow further evaporation. For maximum cooling, your dog broadens the tip of the tongue to increase the surface area available for evaporation. Despite this cooling mechanism, dogs can easily overheat.

Kennel Cough

Canine infectious tracheobronchitis (kennel cough) is one of the most prevalent infectious diseases in dogs. Fortunately, the majority of cases are not serious, resolving on their own in one to two weeks. But because some dogs develop life-threatening complications, you should take precautions to prevent your pet from becoming infected with this highly contagious disease.

Kennel cough can be caused by a number of different airborne bacteria (such as Bordetella bronchiseptica) and viruses (such as canine parainfluenza). Typically, more than one of these pathogens (disease-causing agents) must bombard the dog at once to trigger illness. Such a multifaceted attack is most likely to occur when a dog spends time in close quarters with many other dogs. Dogs who attend dog shows, travel frequently, or stay at kennels have a higher risk of developing kennel cough than do their stay-at-home brethren.

The primary sign of kennel cough is a dry-sounding, spasmodic cough caused by pathogens that induce inflammation of the trachea (windpipe) and bronchi (air passages into the lungs). At the end of a coughing spell, a dog will often retch and cough up a white foamy discharge. Some dogs also develop conjunctivitis (inflammation of the membrane lining the eyelids), rhinitis (inflammation of the nasal mucous membrane), and a nasal discharge. Affected dogs usually remain active and alert and continue to eat well. But if you suspect your dog has kennel cough, isolate the animal from other dogs and call your veterinarian.

Your veterinarian can typically diagnose kennel cough from a physical exam and history. "The cough is very characteristic and can be easily elicited by massaging the dog's larynx or trachea," explains Dr. Gail Mason, an internal medicine specialist in Brunswick, Maine. But if the dog is depressed, feverish, expelling a thick yellow or green discharge from the nose, or making abnormal lung sounds, your veterinarian may want to perform diagnostic tests such as a complete blood count (CBC), chest radiograph (X-ray), and laboratory analysis of the microorganisms inhabiting your dog's airways. These tests can help determine whether the animal has developed pneumonia (a bacterial infection of the lower respiratory tract) or another infectious illness such as canine distemper.

"Most patients seem to be significantly improved with the administration of antibiotics, so I feel that bacteria are part of the disease in most dogs," says Tufts' Dr. Stone. Antibiotics aren't necessary in mild cases because they tend to resolve without medical intervention.

Dr. Stone cautions against administering a cough suppressant without veterinary advice because differentiating between tracheobronchitis and pneumonia can be difficult. "Patients with pneumonia need their cough reflex to clear material from their lungs," he says. "If the cough is inadvertently suppressed in a patient with pneumonia, worsening of the patient's condition could result."

Immunization can be an important part of a kennel-cough prevention program. But since the illness is caused by multiple organisms—making effective immunization difficult—you should focus on minimizing your dog's exposure to the disease-causing organisms themselves. Don't share your dog's toys or food and water bowls with unfamiliar dogs. And if your dog is in an indoor kennel or show, make sure the indoor area is adequately ventilated so airborne organisms are transferred outside.

If your dog is diagnosed with kennel cough, your veterinarian will likely prescribe waiting it out—"tincture of time." But in the case of puppies (especially small-breed pups), very old dogs, immunocompromised dogs, or dogs who have another respiratory ailment, your veterinarian may prescribe antibiotics to ward off complications.

Airborne Allergies

Dogs can develop allergies to many inhalant allergens. Unlike humans, they are more likely to scratch than sneeze. While you sniffle and sneeze your way through summer, your dog may be scratching for the very same reason—seasonal allergies. "Itching is the hallmark of allergies in dogs," says Dr. Gene H. Nesbitt, consulting dermatologist for Tufts Dermatology and Allergy Service.

Seasonal allergies cause respiratory ills in people but in dogs, inhalant allergies trigger itchy skin (pruritus) and the corresponding scratching, licking, or rubbing of troublesome areas. These usually are on the stomach and chest, the legs, and the face and ears. Allergies are also a common cause of inflamed ears (otitis externa) in dogs. As the irritation and scratching become more intense, redness, hair loss, darkened skin pigmentation, sores, and crusting may result and frequently lead to secondary infections.

Atopy, allergic inhalant dermatitis, and atopic disease are all terms veterinarians use to describe this hypersensitization to substances that are inhaled or absorbed through the skin.

Substances that cause an allergic reaction (allergens) include pollens from grass, trees and weeds; mold; dust and dust mites; animal danders; and kapok, a natural fiber. An affected dog very often becomes sensitized to multiple allergens. The condition generally worsens as a dog ages and may progress from a seasonal allergy to a year-round condition. This occurs in about half of affected dogs.

There are regional variations. An atopic dog in Florida or another tropical area may have year-round exposure to pollens and a year-round itch. However, a dog in New England or another area with a temperate climate may be affected only during warmer months. Regardless of the season or where the dog lives, mold, dust and dust mites, and other airborne allergens can also be the cause of year-round allergies.

Under normal circumstances, an animal's immune system mobilizes against specific disease-causing foreign substances, such as viruses and bacteria. But an allergy is the immune system's inappropriate over-response to an otherwise harmless substance. It's generally thought that affected dogs have an inherited predisposition to develop allergies.

Following the initial encounter with a substance, an animal becomes sensitized to the particular allergen, triggering formation of antibodies (immunoglobulin E, or IgE) that attach to specialized connective tissue cells called mast cells and to blood cells called basophils.

When a dog next encounters the particular allergen or group of allergens, the mast cells and basophils respond by releasing powerful chemicals such as histamines that make the skin itch. Each animal has an individual allergy threshold up to which it can tolerate a certain amount of allergen before becoming pruritic, or itchy.

As much as 15 percent of the canine population is affected by inhalant allergies, which typically begin when a dog is from one to three years old.

Susceptible Breeds

Although atopy is seen in almost all breeds, certain breeds appear more susceptible, according to Dr. Nesbitt. These breeds include the Beagle, Boston Terrier, Cairn Terrier, Shar-Pei, Dalmatian, English Bulldog, English Setter, Golden Retriever, Irish Setter, Lhasa Apso, Miniature Schnauzer, Pug, Scottish Terrier, Sealyham Terrier, West Highland White Terrier, and Wire-Haired Terrier.

On the other hand, the American Cocker Spaniel, Dachshund, Doberman Pinscher, German Shepherd, and Poodle appear to have a lower frequency of inhalant allergies.

Making a Diagnosis

"The most important part of a diagnosis is talking with the client," Dr. Nesbitt says. Your veterinarian will want to know as much as possible about when and where the condition started and how it has progressed. He or she will also want to do a physical exam to compare the clinical signs and lesions to the history you have provided. Dr. Nesbitt says atopic dogs are usually observed as "face rubbers, foot lickers, and/or armpit scratchers."

There is no single diagnostic test for inhalant allergies. To make a diagnosis of atopy, your veterinarian may want to rule out other possible causes of the dog's itching. He or she may take hair and tissue samples to screen for differential diagnoses, including fleas and flea allergy, food allergy, or conditions such as sarcoptic mange. He or she also may also prescribe low-dosage prednisone to determine if the condition is a cortisone-responsive allergy.

Management, Not Cures

Keep in mind that your dog's allergic threshold is not a fixed number; it's a combination of many variables that you can help control. Avoidance of allergens is the best solution–though not often a practical one–for canine inhalant allergies.

You can help limit your dog's exposure by keeping the animal indoors when the pollen and mold indexes are high. Your veterinarian can give you some common practical tips on managing your dog's environment, such as maintaining the relative humidity of your house to 30 percent to limit mold and mildew growth. Air conditioners or HEPA air cleaners may help. And the problem may be inside your house—houseplants are a common source of mold.

To help break the dog's "itch-scratch cycle," your veterinarian will probably also prescribe a topical medication (such as 1 percent hydrocortisone) or an oral antihistamine (such as chlorpheniramine or diphenhydramine) for itch relief. Some dogs respond better to one antihistamine than another, so you may need to try several before finding the best control. A short-term course with an oral corticosteroid (such as prednisone) may also be prescribed. If the dog's scratching leads to secondary skin infection, your veterinarian may recommend oral or topical antibiotics as well.

All atopic dogs generally benefit from the soothing effects of a cool bath (warm water makes the itching worse!), with a colloidal oatmeal shampoo and/or conditioner. Bathing not only helps relieve the itch, but it also removes allergens from the skin through which they also can be absorbed.

When your dog's clinical signs last four months or more, or when topical or oral medications have little effect or produce side effects, your veterinarian may suggest doing blood tests (RAST or ELISA) or intradermal skin tests (ID) to pinpoint specific allergens for hyposensitization therapy.

According to Dr. Nesbitt, skin testing is the most widely accepted means of identifying specific allergens. Although blood testing may be more readily available to dog owners, the results are less specific because of possible cross-reactions among allergens. The cost of both tests is about the same.

"Regardless of the test, a 'positive' result doesn't give you a definite diagnosis," Dr. Nesbitt says. "You still need to see a strong correlation of the history and clinical signs with the test results." For example, if a dog has a history of scratching in the summer but doesn't react to pollens when tested, the correlation is poor for seasonal atopy.

Not all veterinarians perform intradermal tests, so your veterinarian may refer you to a board-certified dermatologist at a specialty practice or teaching hospital.

Performing an ID Skin Test

Certain medications, including antihistamines, tranquilizers, and corticosteroids such as prednisone, can interfere with intradermal test results. So, before testing, dogs need to be taken off these medications for the recommended withdrawal times, which can range from several days to several weeks.

In preparation for ID testing, the veterinarian first gives the dog a mild sedative and clips the hair from the test site on the animal's side. Following a grid-like pattern, he or she then injects small amounts of as many as forty to fifty allergens that may include a variety of pollens, animal danders, molds, kapok, dust, and dust mites into individual sites in the top layer of the skin. Within fifteen to thirty minutes, the veterinarian evaluates the test by looking for hives indicating a positive reaction to a particular allergen. Each reaction is graded subjectively according to size, color, and rigidity.

Hyposensitization Therapy

Armed with the results of the intradermal tests, your veterinarian can develop a vaccine(s) tailored to your dog's allergies. The goal of hyposensitization is to reduce the dog's allergic response by injecting it with increasing doses of the allergens.

Although the therapy does not produce a cure, Dr. Nesbitt says that about three out of every four dogs who are treated experience from "excellent" to "fair" results, beginning within a few weeks or months after initiating treatment.

After the early "loading" phase in the first one to two months, your dog will require weekly or monthly "maintenance" injections for the rest of his or her life. Most veterinarians like to teach their clients how to administer the vaccines to make it both more convenient and cost-effective. Dr. Nesbitt says that more than 90 percent of his clients give their own dogs' allergy injections. "One key to success is frequent communication between the owner and the veterinarian," Dr. Nesbitt says. "Allergy treatment is highly individualized and requires micromanagement so as to know when and how to vary the dosage or frequency of treatment."

New Dietary Therapy

In recent years, veterinarians and dog owners have seen and heard much about the positive effects of feeding fatty-acid dietary supplements to atopic dogs. Veterinarians have noted a reduction in itching by from 20 to 40 percent of dogs receiving the supplements.

Fatty acids are thought to compete with arachadonic acid, which triggers itching. Supplements containing omega-3 and omega-6 fatty acids are sold as capsules and liquids, and certain commercial dog foods also contain these fatty acids.

However, there is some controversy among veterinarians over fatty acid supplementation, Dr. Nesbitt says. This is because little is known about how the two should be balanced to get the maximum benefits. He explains that omega-3 is associated with chemicals that are less inflammatory, while omega-6 is associated with chemicals that are more inflammatory.

"As an adjunct to other therapies, fatty acid supplementation may be one more tool to help manage atopic dogs," Dr. Nesbitt says.

Missing: One Bark

Laryngeal paralysis is a common condition that most often develops in middle-aged and older dogs of large or giant breeds. It is a condition in which damage—often for no known reason—occurs to the recurrent laryngeal nerve in a dog's larynx, or voice box.

Raspy breathing, excessive panting, and a gagging cough while eating or drinking are among the symptoms that drive dog owners to seek veterinary advice. Usually, the signs become noticeable as the weather warms.

"Essentially, these dogs struggle to inhale," says Dr. John Berg, chair of Tufts' Department of Clinical Sciences.

The problem takes place in the cartilages located on either side of the windpipe opening. A voice box consists of two tissue folds called arytenoid cartilages. They normally open when the dog inhales. They're also supposed to close while eating or drinking so that water or food won't go down the trachea, or windpipe. But the folds of dogs with laryngeal paralysis don't open and close properly. The dogs are at risk of overheating—and possible death—in hot weather as they must work extra hard to breathe.

One study found 25 percent of dogs undergoing anesthesia for unrelated reasons had some degree of laryngeal paralysis, which can be acquired or inherited.

If the case is mild, a diet and medication, along with avoidance of strenuous exercise and heat, may be all that are needed to manage the condition. These steps can at least delay the need for surgery to widen the larynx's opening. ■

10

Eye Disorders

Your dog's eyes are complex sensory organs that are vulnerable to injury and disease.

E ye problems characterized by redness, discharge, squinting, and sudden vision loss are quite obvious. But some eye ailments are insidious. For example, the early signs of glaucoma (excessive eyeball pressure)—subtle pupil dilation and slight enlargement of the eye and its associated blood vessels—are easy to miss. However, these anomalies can be detected through routine eye exams, which generally require only drops to numb the eye and dilate the pupil, not sedation or general anesthesia.

To measure tear production, veterinarians pass a strip of absorbent paper over the dog's lower eyelid (Schirmer tear test). A drop of fluorescein stain "lights up" corneal scratches, and an ophthalmoscope brings the dog's retina, optic nerve, and ocular blood vessels into focus. In addition, handheld tonometers help veterinarians measure eyeball pressure. Your veterinarian may refer you to a board-certified veterinary ophthalmologist who has sophisticated tools at his or her disposal, including the electroretinogram, which measures the retina's electrical response to light.

Outside Influences

Conjunctivitis is inflammation of the membrane lining the eyelid and the white of the eye (sclera) that has a variety of causes. These include inadequate lubrication (dry eye) due to malfunctioning tear

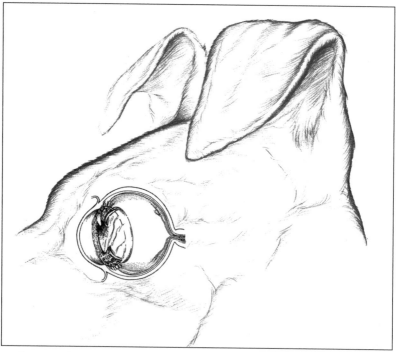

A dog's eye has two chambers (the anterior chamber and the posterior chamber(, separated by a lens. Behind the posterior chamber is the retina, which absorbs the transmitted light and sends neurological signals to the brain.

glands or facial-nerve damage that blocks the blinking reflex. Infection and irritants such as grass, dirt, and smoke also commonly contribute. If the insult damages the cornea—the eye's transparent outer surface—inflammation (keratitis) or a painful corneal ulcer may develop.

Ailments affecting the retina can lead to either gradual or sudden vision loss. Retinal bleeding can result from hemangiosarcoma (a blood-vessel tumor), high blood pressure, a shortage of platelets (blood-clotting components), or ingestion of warfarin (found in some rat poisons). Tumors (such as lymphoma), high blood pressure, and certain systemic fungal infections can cause retinal detachment, separation of the inner layers of the retina from the back of the eye.

Nuclear sclerosis is a normal age-related hardening of the light-focusing lens that develops in dogs at around age seven. Nuclear sclerosis is not a serious impairment, although your dog's close-range vision may be affected. It typically appears as a bluish haze and is sometimes confused with cataracts, a denser lens opacity that significantly impairs vision. Cataracts appear like a crystal or solid rock and most often affect dogs with diabetes mellitus (a condition marked by high blood-sugar levels, which can damage the lens) or young purebred dogs who inherit a genetic flaw.

Faulty genes are also the root cause of progressive retinal atrophy (PRA), an inexorable degeneration of retinal cells to which several breeds including Irish Setters, Labrador Retrievers, and Poodles are predisposed.

Treatment: Simple to Sophisticated

Treatment for eye ailments can range from simple removal of foreign material and administration of infection-fighting drugs to complex surgery. Cyclosporine ointment stimulates tear production for treatment of dry eye. To remove cataracts, veterinary ophthalmologists use phacoemulsification, an ultrasound technique that shatters the damaged lens and removes the pieces.

Treatments for glaucoma include medications to decrease eyeball pressure and surgery to drain fluid from within the eye. In the future, drugs that block the amino acid glutamate may help treat the nerve damage glaucoma causes.

In cases of retinal detachment or hemorrhage, vision is sometimes restored after veterinarians treat the underlying problem—such as high blood pressure. One form of retinal detachment that occurs in purebred German Shepherds and shepherd mixes responds dramatically to treatment with systemic corticosteroids.

Applying Eye Medication

- *Ask if the medication your dog needs comes in drop form. Drops are easier to apply than ointments.*

- *Tip your dog's nose upward so the animal will reflexively look down; this may give you a better target.*

- *Bring your hand over the top of your dog's head from behind so the animal is less likely to draw away or blink when you apply the medication.*

- *Remember, typically, you only need to get one drop or ¼-inch of ointment into your dog's eyes.*

Evading Eye Disorders

You can't prevent all canine eye ailments, but you can increase your dog's chances of trouble-free vision:

■ *Keep chemicals (shampoo!) away from your dog's eyes.*

■ *Keep your dog's head inside moving vehicles.*

■ *Carefully control a diabetic dog's blood-sugar levels.*

■ *Schedule regular eye exams for dogs with chronic eye ailments such as glaucoma.*

■ *Before adopting a purebred puppy, make sure the parents' eyes have been cleared through the Canine Eye Registry Foundation (CERF). Keep in mind, however, that CERF clearance does not guarantee lifelong ocular health since some eye diseases crop up after CERF evaluation.*

■ *Don't breed dogs who carry eye-disease genes. A blood test is available to identify Irish Setters who carry the gene for progressive retinal atrophy, and similar tests for other breeds are under development.*

Prevention

Applying common sense is the soundest strategy for preventing eye problems. Always keep your dog's head inside moving vehicles, check your dog's eyes on a regular basis, and make sure your pet's annual veterinary checkup includes an eye exam. Seek veterinary help for eye problems as soon as you notice them.

If you're considering adding a purebred puppy to your family, ask your veterinarian if inherited eye problems are common in the breed in which you're interested. Select a breeder who routinely has a veterinary ophthalmologist test parents and puppies and submits the data to the Canine Eye Registry Foundation (CERF). CERF collects and disseminates information about breed-specific eye disease in an effort to curb genetically transmitted ocular conditions.

Sudden Blindness

Sudden acquired retinal degeneration syndrome, or SARDS, can rob dogs of their sight overnight. Researchers aren't sure what leads to SARDS; unlike other retinal diseases, such as progressive retinal atrophy, it's inherited. It involves the destruction of the retina's visual cell layer—the rods and cones—resulting in blindness.

However, researchers know that sudden death of neural cells has been associated with a phenomenon called apoptosis. Genes within cells govern cell division and cell death. They remain quiet until chemical messengers set them off. In SARDS, an unknown trigger sets off massive apoptosis of the rods and cones.

SARDS is characterized by acute, or sudden, vision loss. "The dog can be chasing butterflies one second and be blind in the next second," says Dr. Isabel-Ricarda Jurk, assistant professor and ophthalmologist at Tufts University School of Veterinary Medicine. The onset also may be slower, with blindness progressing within one to two weeks. The dog may show a short history of weight gain, with increased appetite, thirst and urination before the onset of SARDS, she says.

Dogs of any breed may be affected, although patients typically are middle-aged or older and more are females. Stress, such as a new house, a new baby or new pet in the house, or boarding, seems to be a factor.

"Since the loss of vision is so abrupt, it is usually harder for these patients to adopt to their new life," Dr. Jurk says. "But once adapted, they do great and still enjoy a great quality of life."

Cataracts

The lens of your dog's eye is normally transparent, but cataracts transform it into a milky, opaque barrier to clear vision. One of the most recent developments in cataract removal is phacoemulsifica-

" A BLIND DOG IN ITS OWN ENVIRONMENT CAN BE A VERY HAPPY DOG, PROVIDED IT RECEIVES FOOD, SECURITY, AND LOVE. "

tion, a gift from human ophthalmology.

During a "phaco," the veterinary ophthalmologist breaks up the cataractous lens with high-frequency sound waves while simultaneously irrigating the eye and removing the lens material with an aspirator. Phacoemulsification requires a smaller incision and involves less trauma than other lens-removal procedures. Dogs recover quicker and more comfortably with fewer postoperative complications.

However, some eye inflammation (uveitis) is inevitable after any cataract surgery, according to Dr. Alan Bachrach, a veterinary ophthalmologist in Lincoln, Massachusetts. "When lens protein enters other parts of the eye, the dog's immune system sets up an inflammatory response, as if the cells were a foreign protein," he says. But because the two- to four-minute phaco involves constant irrigation and suction, less lens protein escapes, thereby minimizing inflammation.

Phaco candidates should be in good health because the procedure requires general anesthesia. The ophthalmologist must also assure that a dog has a healthy retina before recommending a phaco, because all the light in the world won't allow your dog to see unless the retina is functioning.

In evaluating phaco candidates, ophthalmologists also consider lens hardness, which increases as dogs age. Because harder lenses take longer to break up, ophthalmologists usually recommend traditional lens extraction rather than phacoemulsification for dogs with very hard lenses.

After surgery, owners must apply antibiotic and anti-inflammatory eye drops, a procedure as important as the surgery itself. So dogs amenable to postoperative care obviously make better phaco candidates.

Despite its advantages, phacoemulsification never restores "perfect" vision. But even "post-phaco" dogs without lenses can see (although images appear larger) because the remaining intact cornea provides lens-like focusing power.

Some owners opt against phaco because of possible postoperative complications (including detached retinas and excessive eye pressure known as glaucoma), the risks of anesthesia, and high cost. "There's no right or wrong decision about phacos or other elective cataract surgery," Dr. Bachrach says. "A sightless dog's hearing, sense of smell, and touch compensate very well. A blind dog in its own environment can be a very happy dog, provided it receives food, security, and love."

Despite an owner's best efforts to head off eye problems, some dogs do go blind, often very gradually. However, Dr. Bruce Fogle, a London-based veterinarian and author of *The Dog's Mind*, points out that "vision is not as overwhelmingly important for dogs as it is for people." In fact, vision-impaired dogs in familiar surroundings can usually move around comfortably, relying on their powerful senses of smell and hearing.

What blind dogs need most is a caring owner—a "seeing eye person"—who can keep the blind dog's home environment as stable and predictable as possible. If your dog is blind, always supervise the animal when outdoors and don't rearrange the furniture. And if you take your dog off his or her home turf, use a short lead and gentle voice commands to direct your pet's movements.

Lastly, remember when you gaze into your dog's eyes seeking solace, inspiration, or assurance that you are loved, return the favor: look for signs of eye trouble, and if something seems amiss, call your veterinarian.

For More Information

■ *Owners of Blind Dogs:* **www.blinddogs.com**

■ *American College of Veterinary Ophthalmology:* **www.acvo.com/public/op_links.htm**

■ *Veterinary Ophthalmology Information Center, Eyevet Consulting Services:* **www.eyevet.ca**

■ *Iowa State University College of Veterinary Medicine:* **www.vetmed.iastate.edu/services/vth/clinical/ophth/diseases.asp** ■

11

Lend Us Your Ears

If you can see dirt or grit inside your dog's ears, it's time for a cleaning, or possibly a trip to the veterinarian.

Trying to get a good look inside your dog's ears can ignite a battle of wills if he or she prefers petting and playing to poking and prodding. But it's important that you check out the outer part of your dog's ears, because if problems exist there, your pet may have an internal ear problem that requires prompt veterinary attention.

"The main things people at home are going to find are odor, redness and a discharge or accumulation of debris on the inside of the ear flap," says Dr. Gene Nesbitt, consulting dermatologist with Tufts Dermatology and Allergy Service. "These are all the results of underlying conditions. One of the most common problems is yeast and bacteria, or both and, if they go unattended, you'll get an infection. That causes more wax production and provides a medium for the creation of even more yeast and bacteria."

Ear mites, parasitic insects, are another cause for concern. Young dogs in group settings, such as shelters and pet stores, are more likely to have this problem than adults. Frontline or Revolution, ordinarily applied for fleas and ticks, can be an effective treatment when used with a mitacide to kill mites in the ear canal.

Starting Early

A strong first step in health maintenance is observation, but dogs don't always want to cooperate. Dr. Alice Moon-Fanelli, a certified applied animal behaviorist at Tufts University School of Veterinary Medicine, stresses it's important to start early to prevent the problem.

"Ideally, dogs should be desensitized to handling beginning when they are young puppies," she says. "Owners should pay particular attention to stroking the ears and paws and pair the handling with a positive experience. Click and treat training is an ideal method to desensitize adult dogs to accept and enjoy handling for examination and treatment."

Cleaning

If an examination shows only a small amount of wax, you can do the cleaning yourself, Dr. Nesbitt says. No method or tool works better than others, but take care to make sure you don't injure your dog.

"Some dogs have a lot of cracks and crevices at the base of the ear, so a Q-tip would be helpful in that area. Otherwise, it's not recommended that an owner use it to clean deep inside the ear because, if there is any debris in there, you'll just cram it down further," Dr. Nesbitt says. "A good rule of thumb is to not try and clean something you can't see."

Numerous over-the-counter products are intended for ear maintenance. If you want to keep things simple, alcohol is a good solvent. Dr. Nesbitt advises using it only on the inside of the ear flap. Otherwise, it can be an irritant.

Loss of Equilibrium

Inner ear infections and the like fall under a broad collection of ailments called vestibular syndrome. The name comes from the vestibular apparatus, the part of the inner ear containing the neurological parts that tell dogs whether they're upright and how to move their legs accordingly. When the vestibular apparatus becomes disturbed, it's difficult for the dog to know which end is up. Owners may perceive terrible trouble is afoot.

In fact, it may be. The diseases and conditions causing vestibular syndrome include ear tumors; brain tumors; encephalitis, an inflammation and infection of the brain; vascular abnormalities, such as blood clots, or a bleeding blood vessel in the brain; head injury; poisons, including some antibiotics; and middle- and inner-ear infections.

Sometimes vestibular syndrome has no apparent cause. "The signs include falling, rolling, head tilt and turn, vomiting, salivating, inappetence, and abnormal eye movements," says Dr. Jay McDonnell, a veterinary neurologist in private practice in Maryland. "I always tell people that vestibular signs are like jumping off a ride at an amusement park when it spins you around."

The vestibular apparatus is made up of two kinds of neurological receptors. One kind detects tumbling and turning; the other, falling and up-down orientation. Both consist of tiny neurological hairs projecting into fluid-filled canals. When the fluid moves, so do the hairs, creating a message that's sent to four vestibular nuclei in the brain stem and then to the cerebellum, the part of the brain that coordinates movement.

If the body is in an abnormal position, such as upside down, the hypothalamus gets a message, inciting conscious awareness of the position. The brain then sends instructions to nerves in the legs, neck, and eyes, so they move in ways that eliminate dizziness. Messages also go to an area of the brain called the "reticular formation," which controls the state of wakefulness. Vestibular stimulation leads to wakefulness. If any of these nerve pathways becomes disturbed, symptoms of vestibular syndrome may result.

The good news: the syndrome isn't life threatening. But because so many possibilities may cause it, it's a good idea to get an affected dog to a veterinarian as soon as possible.

Leave Some Things to the Experts

Dogs with a lot of hair on the inside of the ears, like Poodles, often require more work. Experienced owners can pluck the hair with tweezers or by hand, but Dr. Nesbitt suggests that most people leave this to professionals.

"Groomers or veterinarians are better equipped to handle a situation like this," he says. "When using tweezers in a dog's ears, you can very easily do more harm than good."

Owners should be alert to their dog's head-shaking and ear-scratching, signs of possible infection.

"You may not be able to see everything going on inside the ear, but don't let that stop you," Dr. Nesbitt says. "The bottom line is to get things checked out by a vet right away and to avoid letting the problem go on and on." ■

12

In the Blood

*Learn about two clotting disorders
that could have a significant impact
on your dog's well-being.*

The circulatory system is an amazing thing. The heart pumps blood continuously throughout the body as long as we or our dogs live. Chapter 2 of this book explores canine heart disease problems. This chapter examines a couple of clotting disorders that can affect our dogs and offers tips for coping with the situation. As always, the best advice will come from your own veterinarian.

Von Willebrand's Disease

You may have never heard of von Willebrand's disease (vWD), but it is the most common inherited bleeding disorder in both humans and their canine companions. Between 1 and 2 percent of the human population has vWD. In dogs, it's been found in at least fifty breeds from Scottish Terriers to Dutch Kooikers, and the list is constantly expanding. It's estimated that at least 70 percent of Doberman Pinschers have or are carriers of vWD. Even mixed breeds aren't immune.

Some people may never know they have a vWD dog. "Many dogs live their whole lives with the disease and never have a bleeding problem, because this isn't the only factor involved in blood clotting," says Dr. Linda Ross, associate professor of internal medicine at Tufts University School of Veterinary Medicine.

The disease was first described in humans in the mid-1920s by Dr. Erik von Willebrand. He had been studying a family in which four sisters had serious, spontaneous bleeds and others had bleeding problems. Three of the sisters bled to death before the age of four.

VWD is caused by a defect in a protein called von Willebrand's Factor (vWF), a sticky molecule found mostly in the lining of blood vessels. The protein plays an important role in blood clotting, mainly by helping platelets plug up injuries in the blood vessels. Von Willebrand's Factor serves as a kind of glue, holding the platelets to the blood vessel wall. If the factor is missing or defective, the platelets will slide away.

Type I vWD is the mildest but most widespread form. Dogs produce some vWF, but much less than normal. Type II is the rarest and so far has been identified only in German Shorthaired Pointers or German Wirehaired Pointers. These dogs may produce normal levels of vWF, but the molecule is malformed and doesn't work. Type III, found in about 10 percent of Scottish Terriers, is the most serious variant. These dogs form no vWF and often die young. Teething may be enough to bring on a major bleed, with some cases of teething puppies requiring blood transfusions to save their lives.

Diagnosis

Often, the early warnings of vWD are so subtle that they can be easily ignored. Veterinarians have several ways of diagnosing the disease. Some will clip a toenail to the quick; a neater, less painful method is a simple test called buccal mucosal bleeding time. "You lift up the dog's lip and make a tiny incision and just wait for the bleeding to stop," Dr. Ross says. That test will give an idea of whether the dog is at an increased risk of bleeding, but won't tell if vWD is the cause. The next step is a blood test that measures the levels of the factors. For Type I and Type III, DNA testing is available for twelve breeds.

Treatment

It is vital that owners of a vWD dog guard against injuries, which may rule out activities with a risk of bruising. Obedience training probably would be fine, but agility training may be ruled out. Dr. Ross also suggests avoiding hard chew toys that might cause gum bleeding as well as medications affecting blood clotting, such as aspirin and related drugs and certain antibiotics.

Some supplements also may promote bleeding in a vWD dog, she says. Fish oil supplements, for example, may impair platelet function and should be used cautiously.

"If the dog has vWD, there is very little you can do in the long-term chronic phase, but there are things to do in the short term, if the dog is having surgery, for example," Dr. Ross says. She says it's important to have the dog blood-typed before any surgery in case a transfusion is needed.

In dogs with mild cases, a synthetic hormone called desmopressin acetate (DDAVP) may be all that is needed to raise blood levels of the missing factor. The drug works by releasing vWF from its storage sites.

In some vWD dogs, the tendency to bleed may be associated with hypothyroidism, a condition in which the thyroid produces lower than normal levels of the hormones that regulate metabolism. Hypothyroidism is discussed elsewhere in this chapter.

About PSS

Your dog's liver problems may be related to the circulatory system. It could be that an abnormal blood vessel problem known as portosystemic shunt (PSS) is rerouting blood around the liver instead of through it.

While PSS is relatively uncommon, it can occur in any breed but seems more prevalent in small dogs, especially Yorkshire Terriers and Cairn Terriers.

PSS will make a dog chronically ill. It can lead to death if left untreated, so a dog showing clinical signs of liver dysfunction should be checked for this disorder.

Dietary management and oral antibiotics can help, but surgery is the only way to correct PSS.

About Hypothyroidism

Hypothyroidism is a relatively common canine disorder in which the thyroid gland (two small lobes located on either side of the trachea or windpipe) secretes insufficient thyroid hormones. Fortunately, hypothyroidism isn't life threatening, but it does diminish quality of life. Once diagnosed, the disorder is relatively easy to treat.

Your dog's thyroid gland uses stored iodine (obtained from food) to produce the thyroid hormones that are critical to maintaining his or her normal metabolic rate, the rate at which the body converts nutrient energy into "fuel." If the thyroid gland degenerates or becomes inflamed, it can no longer produce sufficient quantities of hormones.

While all owners should be on the lookout for changes in their dog's appearance or behavior that suggest hypothyroidism (unexplained weight gain, lethargy, mental dullness and hair or skin abnormalities), owners of middle-aged dogs or genetically predisposed dogs should be especially watchful. If you notice any signs, consult your veterinarian. Treatment typically involves a supplemental thyroid hormone that is given orally. Once thyroid levels have stabilized within a normal range, your veterinarian will likely check the levels at your dog's yearly exam.

Hemophilia

Hemophilia is one of the few sex-linked traits that affect dogs. It's the most common hereditary coagulation factor defect found in dogs, cats and people. Dogs inherit it in the same genetic way people do. It's carried by females but tends to affect mostly males. It is an X-linked, recessive disorder. Males only have one X chromosome, so male dogs are either affected or free of it. Females have two X chromosomes, so they can be affected, free, or a carrier with no clinical signs. Affected dogs and carriers should not be bred. Owners of dogs with a mild form of the disease may never know their pet suffers from hemophilia unless the animal has surgery or experiences a trauma.

Clotting factors in the blood are referred to as Factors I through XIII. Factor VIII is critical to form normal blood clots, and is deficient in hemophilia A. Hemophilia B is more severe, and dogs with that condition have low Factor IX activity.

Diagnosis

Affected males are easy to diagnose, says Dr. Michael Stone, assistant clinical professor of internal medicine at Tufts. "First a screening test, an APTT, or activated partial thromboplastin time,

❝ GERMAN SHEPHERDS ARE MOST
COMMONLY PREDISPOSED AND AFFECTED,
BUT HEMOPHILIA CAN OCCUR IN OTHER
BREEDS AND MIXES. ❞

is performed, then a specific measurement of clotting factor activity may be performed to confirm the type of hemophilia. If the APTT test is normal, the patient doesn't have hemophilia. If positive, the patient may have hemophilia A or B, or some other less common form.

"In males, the test is easily interpreted as positive or negative. The ability of the available tests to determine if a female is unaffected or a carrier is limited, however, due to the wide variability of clotting factor activity in normal patients."

With mild forms of hemophilia, excessive bleeding may be the only sign, noticed after major trauma or surgery, Dr. Stone says. "With moderate disease, severe bleeding occurs after surgery or major injury; some bleeding occurs after minor trauma, with occasional bleeding into joints—causing lameness—or spontaneous bleeding without obvious trauma. With severe disease, prolonged bleeding may occur after injury. Even without obvious trauma, spontaneous bleeding may occur into joints and muscles, causing signs of lameness. The loss of a large amount of blood into the chest or abdomen may cause signs of sudden weakness."

German Shepherds are most commonly predisposed and affected, but hemophilia can occur in other breeds and mixes. Vaccination may temporarily lower the blood platelet count and predispose the dog to bleeding, Dr. Stone says.

Treatment

Treatment options for hemophiliacs are limited, Dr. Stone says. "Transfusions of clotting factors from normal dogs may be administered until bleeding has stopped. With moderately and mildly affected patients, avoiding trauma along with intermittent transfusions as needed may allow long-term survival. However, patients with severe disease are often euthanized because of the inability to successfully control their disease. Some drugs may be tried in the less severely affected patients; however, no veterinary studies have shown benefit of any drug."

Hematomas, masses of clotted blood, can form in hemophiliacs for many reasons, such as needle use or minor traumas. To treat them, veterinarians can use a clotting factor concentrated in the form of cryoprecipitate—a frozen form of Factor VIII—when available, says Dr. Jean Dodds, a veterinarian in Garden Grove, California, who owns Hemopet, a nonprofit animal blood bank. "Hemophilia B is treated with the supernatant plasma (cryoprecipitate and plasma frozen together) after the cryoprecipitate is removed or with whole, fresh-frozen plasma. If the patient is also significantly anemic from bleeding, packed red blood cells would be given as well.

"If cryoprecipitate is not available, whole fresh-frozen plasma or even whole blood can be used, but therapy is not as good at controlling the hemorrhage quickly, and residual body damage or malfunction can result. If the hematoma doesn't go down in size quickly, it can impair function of the affected tissue area," she says. "Of course, for these animals, only blood type-matched or compatible universal donor blood components should be used."

Many owners choose to euthanize hemophiliac dogs. The cost of treatment is significant, emergencies frequent, and the emotional strain wearing. Some people donate their hemophiliac dogs to research facilities like the veterinary school at Cornell University in Ithaca, New York. Cornell's school has a clinical diagnostic lab for hemophiliacs and conducts research to identify mutations causing hemophilia and tracks mutations in hopes of assisting future generations of dogs. ■

13

Skin Problems

---

*Itchy skin can be traced to a variety
of causes, many of which interact
with, or resemble, one another.*

Itchy skin (pruritus) can be traced to allergies, parasites, bacterial and fungal infections, and hereditary skin defects among other causes. And because many of these itchy disorders interact with or resemble one another, ferreting out the source of the problem and treating it can prove difficult.

If your dog has the itchies, he or she is not alone. "It is estimated 10 to 15 percent of the canine population is infected with airborne allergies," says Dr. Gene Nesbitt, consulting dermatologist with Tufts Dermatology and Allergy Service. "Food allergies may account for up to 1 percent of all canine dermatoses, or skin diseases, in general practices and about 10 percent of all canine allergic skin diseases, excluding parasite allergy."

The Skin

Your dog's skin is a three-layered organ consisting of the outer epidermis, middle dermis, and inner subcutis. The skin provides your dog with protection and pouchlike receptacles (follicles) for the animal's hair coat. The skin also plays an important role in regulating body temperature and storing water and fat.

The skin is the outermost line of defense in your dog's immune system. The epidermis's leathery-walled keratinocyte cells migrate from "birth" at the base of the epidermis to death at the skin surface. There, they form a barrier between dog and environment. Keratinocytes and other epidermal cells also secrete proteins such as interferon (which prevents viruses from multiplying) and alert infection-fighting white blood cells to the presence of unfriendly intruders. Dead keratinocytes on the skin's surface also harbor a thriving (usually benign) community of bacteria, some of which ward off invasions from other more harmful organisms.

If the epidermis is the skin's armor plating, the dermis is its plumbing and wiring. Full of blood and lymph vessels, nerves, and connective tissue, the dermis transports nutrients and waste products, helps regulate body temperature (by modulating blood flow), and transmits signals between skin and brain.

The dermis also collaborates with the epidermis to produce follicles, hairs, and their associated sweat glands and sebaceous glands. Sebaceous glands produce a waxy secretion called sebum that lubricates the skin's surface, and sweat glands discharge moisture through hair follicles.

The subcutis is the skin's fat layer. Its plump cells pad and insulate the body and store and produce important substances such as hormones.

You can help your veterinarian identify the cause of your dog's itch by providing information such as when and where the itch started, how it progressed, and what other signs of skin disease you noticed.

ANDREW CUNNINGHAM, TUSVM

The Itch

All dogs scratch periodically (and often follow with a good shake) to clean themselves and stimulate their skin glands. But dogs also scratch in response to an itch—an irritating, localized skin sensation transmitted to the brain. "Excessive scratching or licking is a sign that your dog's itch has pathological [disease-related] origins," says Dr. Laurie Stewart, a dermatologist at Veterinary Dermatology of New England in Westford, Massachusetts.

Itchiness often increases at night as stimulation of the other physical senses wanes. Experts also suspect that boredom and anxiety can amplify itch. And the simple truth is that some dogs itch more than others. "Two breeds or individuals with the same skin problem may have different degrees of itch," observes Dr. Richard Anderson, a retired dermatologist at Angell Memorial Animal Hospital in Boston, Massachusetts.

Secondary Skin Ailments

"A lot of dogs that have allergic disorders also develop secondary skin problems such as bacterial infections," says Dr. Richard Anderson, a retired dermatologist at Boston's Angell Memorial Animal Hospital. A furiously scratching paw can break the skin, allowing bacteria and other organisms to invade and resulting in inflamed, moist lesions called "hot spots" (acute moist dermatitis).

Secondary infections can transform the challenge of diagnosis and treatment into a chicken-or-egg dilemma. "It's important to know whether we're looking at an itch that rashes or a rash that itches," Dr. Anderson says. "If the itch comes first, it's probably an allergy; if the rash comes first, it may be something else."

Itchy Allergies

Allergies—the immune system's overreaction to inhaled, contacted, or ingested substances (called allergens)—are the leading cause of canine itch. Allergens (including foods, pollen, chemicals, and parasite byproducts) abound in the canine environment. In most dogs, these substances produce no reaction. But some dogs do react. Such dogs are genetically predisposed to become hypersensitive to certain allergens after repeated exposure. Allergic reactions in dogs involve the mass release of itch-inducing chemical mediators (such as histamine).

"The amount of discomfort, severity of pruritus—or intense itching—and distribution, severity, and intensity of secondary lesions resulting from pruritus are extremely variable for all causes of allergy," Dr. Nesbitt says.

Flea Bite Allergy

A leading cause of itchy allergies is the pesky flea. The allergen is not the flea itself, but the proteins in the flea's saliva. When a flea bites a hypersensitive dog, the allergens enter the dog's skin, producing a reddish, pimplelike welt. Soon thereafter, the dog develops a persistent, localized itch at the bite site. If fleas remain on the dog, the allergic reaction intensifies, sometimes leading to hair loss, generalized itch, and secondary bacterial infections. In areas where fleas are prevalent, flea hypersensitivity is considered the most common cause of allergy, often occurring with food allergies and atopy, the canine equivalent of hay fever, Dr. Nesbitt says.

Numerous other parasites—including ticks, mites, lice, and worms—can trigger allergic reactions in dogs. Most irritating among these is the tiny Sarcoptes mite, whose burrowing in the outer epidermis produces what is probably the itchiest canine skin disorder, sarcoptic mange. When Sarcoptes mites infiltrate a dog who is hypersensitive to mite feces and byproducts, the animal goes into fits of frenzied scratching, eventually leading to open, yellow-encrusted sores. As long as the mites persist—and they can for years if left untreated—so does the itching, scratching, and skin damage.

Airborne Allergies

Atopy, the canine analog to hay fever, is an allergic reaction to inhaled or absorbed environmental particles such as pollen or dust. Rather than the sneezing, sniffling, and watery eyes humans experience, dogs are overcome with itchy skin, often on the feet, face, or belly. Although atopic itching is usually not accompanied by rashes, it often leads to complications such as thickened or scaly skin and secondary bacterial or yeast infections.

Owners can do their part to reduce their dog's exposure to airborne allergens. They can keep their pets indoors during lawn mowing and high pollen season, keep them out of basements that harbor

> 66 ATOPY, THE CANINE ANALOG TO HAY
> FEVER, IS AN ALLERGIC REACTION TO
> INHALED OR ABSORBED ENVIRONMENTAL
> PARTICLES SUCH AS POLLEN OR DUST. 99

dust and mold, minimize the number of indoor plants, and rinse off their pets after they've been in fields or tall grass. Dr. Nesbitt also recommends using fatty acid supplements as adjunctive therapy for pruritic dogs in consultation with your veterinarian.

Food Allergies

Some dogs also exhibit allergic reactions to certain foods and to fungal and bacterial byproducts. As with atopy, these allergies often cause rashless itching that can lead to secondary complications.

The usual culprits for food allergies are protein sources like beef, chicken, corn, wheat, or soy, but food allergies are rare, says Dr. Linda Ross, associate professor at Tufts University School of Veterinary Medicine. "Food intolerances are much more common. Perhaps it's a semantic difference to some, but a true allergy provokes an immunologic reaction while intolerance (provokes) a non-immunologic reaction," she says.

Blood and skin scratch tests used on people haven't been shown to be helpful in diagnosing food allergies in dogs, Dr. Ross says. "A food elimination trial is still the best method, albeit not the easiest." She advises owners to switch to a novel protein diet, one that includes foods their pets haven't previously eaten, such as venison. Owners must take care not to offer treats, chews, and vitamins while the dog is on the diet.

"The keys are to feed only the new diet and feed it for long enough to know that it is or isn't effective," Dr. Ross says. "This can be up to twelve weeks. Then if the owners want to, they can try adding back in foods to find out which trigger signs. In my experience, most stay on the new diet to avoid problems."

Contact Allergies

Dogs may react to plants, nickel, rubber, plastic, dyes, wool, newsprint, carpeting, carpet fresheners, topical medications, and other substances and objects. Hair loss, itching, and skin changes like thickening and discoloration are signs of contact allergies, the least common type affecting dogs. Dogs with thinly coated areas on their skin may be affected. Removal of the allergen is the long-term solution.

Things That Sting

Bees, wasps, hornets, fire ants, spiders, and scorpions can inject toxic substances into animals through bites or stings. And in warm weather, curious canines often cross paths with these venomous invertebrates.

Dogs usually are stung or bitten on the face and foreleg. Thankfully, most dogs experience only skin redness, swelling, and itchiness at the bite site. Localized reactions usually heal within forty-eight hours. You can help your pet through the healing process by applying cold compresses, a baking soda and water paste, and/or topical or oral anti-inflammatory steroids prescribed by your veterinarian.

Occasionally, a dog has a more severe—and potentially fatal—systemwide allergic reaction (anaphylaxis). Signs of anaphylaxis include widespread swelling or hives, vomiting, loss of muscle coordination, and pale mucous membranes caused by poor blood circulation. Quick veterinary intervention is crucial in these situations. Veterinarians treat anaphylaxis with intravenous fluids and epinephrine to help jump-start the dog's cardiovascular system and restore blood pressure. They inject steroids to calm down the overactive immune system.

As a precaution, always monitor your dog after encounters with things that sting and bite. If the animal has already had one anaphylactic episode, each subsequent episode may be more intense. Some veterinarians instruct owners of sting- and bite-allergic dogs on how to use an EpiPen. Available by prescription at most pharmacies, these devices contain a premeasured dose of injectable epinephrine for emergency administration.

Non-Allergic Itching

Some organisms and substances that are not true allergens trigger itch. Among these is the bacterium Staphylococcus intermedius, a normally benign resident of the skin that can become infectious. Typified by a bumpy rash and itchy, inflamed, hairless patches, Staphylococcus infections often follow on the heels of other disorders such as flea-saliva dermatitis, atopy, and acral lick dermatitis (the condition that results from a behavior disorder characterized by constant licking and chewing of the legs). Staphylococcus can also infect the scaly skin and clogged hair follicles that result from seborrhea or other secretory problems.

Certain fungi can also cause non-allergic itch by invading the skin via soil and infected animals. Some fungi (Microsporum, for example) thread the dog's hair follicles with filaments that give rise to mildly itchy, circular, hairless patches commonly called ringworm. Some yeasts (which are a different type of fungi) produce rashes that are more amorphous. Fungi do the most harm to dogs with preexisting conditions such as immune or nutritional deficiencies or atopy that make them vulnerable to fungal infection.

> " Certain fungi can also cause non-allergic itch by invading the skin via soil and infected animals. "

Diagnosis

You can help your veterinarian identify the cause of your dog's itch by providing information such as when and where the itch started, how it progressed, and what other signs of skin disease you noticed. Your veterinarian or veterinary dermatologist will examine your dog to assess the animal's general condition and look for telltale signs of skin trouble such as rashes or welts. The veterinarian may also take samples of skin, fluid, or hair to test for microscopic evidence of parasites, bacteria, and fungi.

If your veterinarian suspects an allergy, he or she may test your dog's reaction to samples of common allergens injected into the dermis. To check for food allergies, your veterinarian may also suggest eliminating certain foods from your dog's diet. Some diagnostic tests, such as culturing fungi, require specialized laboratory equipment and can take several weeks.

Get Your Dander Up

Folk wisdom celebrates breeds believed to be hypoallergenic, but the truth is that no dogs are. The American Kennel Club notes these breeds have single-layer coats and generally produce less dander than double-coated breeds such as Pomeranians, but warns that reactions to individual dogs vary:

- *Basenji*

- *Bedlington Terrier*

- *Bichon Frise*

- *Chinese Crested*

- *Giant, Standard and Miniature Schnauzer*

- *Italian Greyhound*

- *Irish Water Spaniel*

- *Kerry Blue Terrier*

- *Maltese*

- *Poodle*

- *Portuguese Water Dog*

- *Soft Coated Wheaten Terrier*

- *Xoloitzcuintli*

Prevention and Treatment

Because they often stem from exposure to commonplace substances and organisms, allergic reactions are virtually impossible to completely prevent. The most basic treatment is to isolate your dog from the allergens that cause reactions. For example, your veterinarian may recommend that you eliminate allergenic foods, purge your dog (and the environs) of fleas and mites, and keep him or her inside on "heavy pollen" days. Also, your veterinarian may recommend periodic desensitizing injections of allergens to diminish your dog's allergic reaction and the resulting itch.

If your dog suffers from reactions to ubiquitous or unidentified allergens, your best bet is to break the itch/scratch cycle. Don't underestimate the value of a cool bath; it can bring temporary relief from itching while cleansing the skin of allergens and other contaminants. Corticosteroids (such as Prednisolone), applied to the affected area or ingested orally, can provide effective short-term relief from itching and inflammation, although long-term use can cause side effects that outweigh the benefits. (Always follow your veterinarian's instructions when administering steroidal medications at home.) For long-term itch control during allergy season, veterinarians often prescribe antihistamines and fatty-acid dietary supplements.

The best way to fight itching from non-allergic bacterial and fungal infections is to treat the underlying causes such as flea bites. Veterinarians prescribe an array of ointments, dips, antibiotics, and fungicides to combat secondary fungal and bacterial infections.

In the long run, good canine grooming and meticulous parasite-control efforts can go a long way to help keep your dog's skin in top form. ■

Section III

Bones & Joints

14

Dysplasia

*Dysplasia is a common disorder.
How you treat it early on can have
a big impact on your dog.*

The old German Shepherd had a hard time getting up and walking into the examination room at the veterinary clinic, while the eager Labrador puppy across the room did a little bunny hop with his hind legs as he was led in for an exam. Different breeds, different ages, but unfortunately, both dogs shared the same condition: canine hip dysplasia.

Both dogs exhibited classic symptoms of the condition, which can simply be defined as misalignment of the hip joint. The normal hip joint is a ball and socket joint where the "ball," the femoral head, fits snugly into the "socket," the acetabulum. If there's not a good fit between the ball and socket, the joint becomes loose. Over time, the looseness and poor fit leads to inflammation and bony changes in and around the joint, commonly referred to as arthritis. It is this inflammation of the joint that leads to the clinical signs of lameness and/or pain. The term "dysplasia" itself means abnormal development or growth.

Bunny Hop

A dog with hip dysplasia may be stiff when first rising from a prone position and may have trouble going up or down stairs or jumping, especially into a car or truck (the latter might be particularly difficult due to the height). Dogs with hip dysplasia tire easily; they may sit down in the middle of their walk. An abnormal gait, such as a "bunny hop" with the back legs usually is observed when running or going up stairs, and also may be a sign of hip dysplasia.

Hip dysplasia is very common, according to Dr. Randy Boudrieau, professor of surgery at Tufts University School of Veterinary Medicine. "A significant proportion of large breed dogs may have problems with hip dysplasia," he says. "Not all dogs, however, show clinical signs of the problems." This is the key point in treating hip dysplasia, Dr. Boudrieau notes: "Some dogs are quite stoic, and can run and play despite having relatively severe arthritic changes in their hips. I've seen X-rays of hips that were so bad I wondered how the dog could walk so well; conversely, other dogs cannot tolerate much pain at all despite minimal arthritic changes."

As a concerned owner, don't waste time feeling guilty that you ran too far with your puppy, or that the fall your dog took on the slippery kitchen floor caused his or her hip problems. Hip dysplasia is a hereditary developmental condition. "Dogs either have it or they don't, although certain things may cause more or less expression of the problem—such as nutrition," Dr. Boudrieau says.

Don't "Push" Nutrition

Big dogs are more susceptible than small dogs to hip dysplasia, and some breeds are genetically more predisposed to the condition than others. You should check your puppy's parentage, but even if both parents had good hips, there's still as much as a 20 percent chance the offspring can have bad hips. As noted, nutrition can play a role in the genetic predisposition of this condition. "Pushing" nutrition in puppies susceptible to hip dysplasia causes too rapid a weight gain and an early growth spurt—both of which are detrimental to normal joint development (and other orthopedically related diseases). A puppy diet too high in calories and protein that stimulates rapid growth or a "free choice" (unlimited access to food) diet contributes to abnormal joint development, the most common example of which is hip dysplasia. "Some people think that by feeding a

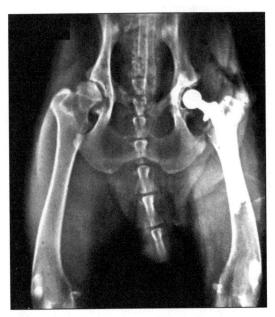

Note the poor fit of the ball and socket in this X-ray of a dog with hip dysplasia. This poor fit can lead to arthritic inflammation that will hamper the dog's movement and potentially cause serious pain. This dog has had a total hip replacement on one hip and signs of dysplasia in the other hip.

puppy lots of protein, it will grow bigger," Dr. Boudrieau says, "but that's not the case. The puppy will definitely grow faster, with the greater chance to develop joint abnormalities, but will end up the same adult size if fed a more controlled diet."

So it is very important to monitor both the quality and quantity of food your puppy eats for the first year of his or her life; feed your dog the proper amount for his or her size and weight, and don't allow unlimited access to food. "One recommendation is a regular puppy chow for the first two months, then switching to a growth diet (specifically formulated for large breed dogs) until they are a year of age," says Dr. Boudrieau. He says giving your dog extra vitamins or calcium isn't a good idea, either: "A sure way to mess up the balance in his system is with supplementation."

Treatment Choices

Treating your dog's hip dysplasia depends upon the dog's age, the seriousness of the condition, and the kind of lifestyle you or your dog expects. For an overweight dog, the answer may be as simple as a diet. Those extra pounds place a lot of strain on the dog's joints. If the hips are a source of the discomfort due to the arthritic changes, the added weight can magnify the pain. Helping your dog to lose weight with a

> " EXERCISE—NOT ENOUGH OR TOO
> MUCH—CAN EXACERBATE THE ARTHRITIS
> OF HIP DYSPLASIA. "

low-calorie regime may go a long way in helping to manage the pain.

Exercise—not enough or too much—can exacerbate the arthritis of hip dysplasia. If your dog is a couch potato all week and the two of you go on a three-hour hike on Saturday, your pet likely will be in pain by Sunday. Instead, a commonsense approach is to take short walks more often. Your pet may be stiff at first, but generally will feel better once he or she is moving and the joints warm up. Be considerate of your dog's condition—if his or her hips are bad, don't allow the animal to run all over the field to fetch a ball or stick, even though that's exactly what he or she would prefer to do. This doesn't mean you can't play ball with your dog; you just have to set a limit and find a happy medium where the dog will not experience any discomfort after the activity. "Dogs have no common sense," says Dr. Boudrieau, adding that his own Labrador would "run after the ball as many times as I throw it for her."

One good example of this "exercise moderation," as Dr. Boudrieau calls it, was aptly demonstrated by a client who is a runner. "The dog was experiencing problems keeping up with her on her runs, and developing problems by the next day, such as stiffness, difficulty rising, and lameness. We explained that it was just too hard on the dog's arthritic hips to do a long run. So, she did her distance running without him, and took the dog on short jogs instead, and the problem was solved."

Some dogs benefit from swimming. "It's an excellent activity that is something fun you can do with your dog and still relieve the stress to his joints," says Dr. Boudrieau. The only limitations are that not all dogs like to swim, and the weather also may be a restrictive factor.

Managing Pain

Despite the commonsense approach to your dog's discomfort, there certainly will be days that your arthritic dog will still be in pain. These days may be the result of overdoing some form of activity despite your best intentions, or simply may be the result of a change in the weather (damp and rainy days in particular).

Medication

Many dogs' pain and discomfort can be managed quite successfully with an occasional dose of anti-inflammatory medication, such as aspirin. Check with your vet before giving your dog any medication, as even aspirin can cause significant gastrointestinal upset (vomiting and diarrhea). Dr. Boudrieau suggests starting with a buffered aspirin product, such as Ascriptin. "You don't have to give it to the dog every day, only on days when it's clear he's in pain," he says. "The best analogy is to think about your own use when you have a sore back or sore muscles."

For dogs who can't tolerate aspirin (GI upset or gastric ulcers) there are other medications especially formulated for the dog that have fewer such side effects, like Rimadyl manufactured by Pfizer, and EtoGesic by Fort Dodge. "Stay completely away from other commonly used over-the-counter anti-inflammatory medications used for people with arthritis, such as Motrin or Advil," warns Dr. Boudrieau, "as there is a much narrower margin of safety when these products are used in the dog."

Soft Surfaces

Most dogs prefer to lie on a cool surface, such as a tile or cement floor. Unfortunately, the arthritic dog with bad hips will become quite stiff in a short time under such conditions. Encouraging your dog to lie on an insulated dog bed, or orthopedic ("egg crate") mattress will help alleviate these problems.

Heat

Heating pads are a bad idea, and have caused extensive burns in dogs. If you must use heat, try moist heat. This is easily accomplished by placing a small towel or washcloth under hot running water and then wringing it out (it should not be so hot that it is uncomfortable to handle) and placing it over the affected joint. The towel will cool quickly, and so must be reheated periodically. This will provide some temporary relief, and may be used in conjunction with the anti-inflammatory medications when your dog is experiencing pain.

Acupuncture

Acupuncture may be used successfully for pain relief for some dogs. But, again, check with your veterinarian first to make sure there's no other physical problem that's causing your pet's pain.

Vulnerable Breeds

The Orthopedic Foundation for Animals maintains databases of inheritable diseases to help reduce their incidence. The databases list dogs who have been screened by veterinarians for a variety of problems, including patellar luxation and hip dysplasia.

Based on the OFA's official registry, this chart lists the breeds reporting the greatest percentage of elbow dysplasia between January 1974 and December 2003. For more information, visit **www.offa.org**.

Breed Dysplastic	Number of Evaluations	Percent
1. Chow Chow	302	45.7
2. Rottweiler	7,921	41.3
3. Bernese Mountain Dog	5,061	30.1
4. Chinese Shar-Pei	157	27.4
5. Newfoundland	2,876	26.3
6. Fila Brasileiro	123	20.3
7. German Shepherd Dog	19,792	19.8
8. American Bulldog	139	19.4
9. American Staffordshire Terrier	218	16.5
10. Bloodhound	543	16.0
11. English Setter	1,303	16.0
12. Mastiff	3,044	15.5
13. Bullmastiff	1,110	14.1
14. English Springer Spaniel	526	13.7
15. Australian Cattle Dog	230	13.5
16. Greater Swiss Mountain Dog	868	13.0
17. Labrador Retriever	24,090	12.0
18. Gordon Setter	57	11.7
19. Golden Retriever	9,630	11.6
20. Irish Wolfhound	192	10.9

Surgical Alternatives

Surgical alternatives exist to treating hip dysplasia. While they are more aggressive than managing diet and exercise, in some cases they can provide the most effective treatment.

Triple Pelvic Osteotomy

If a puppy has been diagnosed with hip dysplasia and no significant arthritic changes have developed, a triple pelvic osteotomy (TPO) may be performed. This procedure improves the mechanics around the hip joint by re-establishing the good fit of the ball and socket joint. In this procedure, the puppy is anesthetized and an osteotomy of the pelvis (a fracturing of the bone by the surgeon) is performed in three places, freeing the area of the socket so that it can be rotated to fit better with the ball joint. The new position is secured into place with a specially designed plate and screws that allow the bone to heal in the more mechanically advantageous position. Although the surgery sounds complicated, most puppies are up and around again within a couple of days.

There are, however, several important considerations for owners who are contemplating such a procedure for their dog. The surgery generally is done on both hips, and requires four to six weeks of recovery between surgeries and up to two to three months after that before the dog can resume normal activities. "In a six- to seven-month-old puppy, this much restriction of activity takes a fair amount of dedication on the part of the owner," Dr. Boudrieau says.

Femoral Head and Neck Ostectomy & Total Hip Replacement

For older dogs, there are two "salvage" operations available: a femoral head and neck ostectomy (FHO) and a total hip replacement (THR). Both procedures eliminate the affected hip joint to relieve the pain and discomfort associated with the arthritis.

■ Femoral Head and Neck Ostectomy

The "true" salvage procedure is the femoral head and neck ostectomy (FHO). In this procedure, the ball portion of the joint is removed, and the surrounding muscles of the buttocks support the dog's hip—and a "false joint" consisting of scar tissue is formed. This procedure works best in the smaller breeds of dogs since they have less reliance on skeletal support to brace their weight. Despite this apparent limitation, it still is successfully used in the larger breeds of dogs—provided the end result of pain control is the goal. These dogs will, however, continue to show a lameness, and will tire more quickly due to the lack of skeletal support of the hip joint. This is a relatively inexpensive procedure, usually performed for less than a thousand dollars.

■ Total Hip Replacement

The alternative procedure that maintains skeletal support while simultaneously eliminating the arthritic hip joint is the total hip replacement surgery (THR). This procedure is identical to the operation performed in humans. Here, the ball is replaced with a stainless steel (or in some cases titanium) ball and shaft, and the socket is replaced with a polyethylene plastic cup. Most commonly, these prosthetic devices are fixed in place with an acrylic bone cement. Because of the large number and size of the implants and the bone cement, the possibility of infection is the greatest concern with this surgical technique. Numerous additional precautions are used to minimize this potential complication, just as in human hip surgery. As in humans, the implants last about ten to fifteen years and are usually good for the life of the dog.

About ten years ago, a new type of cementless hip prosthesis was being developed for use in dogs. Despite initial promising results, the system didn't become readily available for many years as it was being tested. The new implant, made of titanium, was developed to have the stem secured into the proximal femur—the upper thighbone—with screws and a new cup that replaced the socket with a "press-fit" into the bone.

The implant offers several advantages. Because of its roughened surface, healthy bone eventually grows into it, forming a more natural biological union. This reduces the chances of infection and of the artificial hip loosening over time.

Despite using the cementless prosthesis almost exclusively, Dr. Boudrieau still describes the cemented hip as the gold standard because it has been in use for so long. "We offer both the cemented and cementless implant at Tufts, but I prefer the cementless," he says. "It's still new, so we tell owners we don't have the long-term data yet to confirm its potential long-term benefits. However, the data we have so far are very promising."

Although some dogs may appear to need both hips replaced based upon X-ray evaluation of their arthritic hips, the surgical technique is based upon clinical function. "In our experience, over 90 percent of the dogs do well enough after a single hip replacement that the other hip need not be replaced," Dr. Boudrieau says. The dog's function on the new hip can be expected to approach normal after a prosthetic replacement.

Selection of the most appropriate surgical candidate for a THR is based upon clinical dysfunction and a failure to respond adequately to appropriate medical management. Most dogs are six to eight years old when this technique is performed. It can also be performed on younger dogs, but they must be skeletally mature (at least a year old). There is also a risk that the implant can become loose over time when placed in such a young animal. Although this occurrence is uncommon, it is the rationale for delaying the procedure to older animals whenever possible.

On the opposite end of the spectrum, a THR in a very old dog will likely meet limited success due to the advanced age and likely lesser overall strength and robust status of the patient. The analogy here, Dr. Boudrieau says, "is the difference in having your grandmother's hip replaced at either sixty or ninety years old. You would expect her to handle the anesthesia and surgery with fewer problems, and have a significantly better result at the younger age."

The major drawback to this procedure is the expense, which can run at least thirty-five hundred dollars per hip.

"This is something people need to think about long and hard," Dr. Boudrieau says. "Just because a dog has bad hips does not mean a THR has to be done. If the dog is functioning OK, it's not necessary. The key is whether or not the dog is having any clinical dysfunction.

Elbow Dysplasia

Elbow dysplasia doesn't get the same word of mouth as hip dysplasia, but it's as serious and even more complicated, said Karl Kraus, Tufts orthopedic surgery professor. "If you compare it to patellar luxation [in which the kneecap slips out of place] or to hip dysplasia, it's another dimension of complexity because it has to do with the way the three bones of the elbow come together," Dr. Kraus says. "Because of that, there's a lot of variability in the manifestation of elbow dysplasia from one patient to the next and in different degrees of dysplasia, even from breed to breed."

Elbow dysplasia affects the forelegs only, Dr. Kraus says. He characterizes the disorder as congenital. It occurs when the three elbow bones—the radius, ulna, and humerus–don't develop at the same rate or don't fit together perfectly.

> 66 ALTHOUGH THE DISORDER
> MAY BE DIAGNOSED IN ONE ELBOW,
> THERE'S A GOOD CHANCE IT'S ALSO
> PRESENT BILATERALLY... 99

It's difficult to calculate the incidence of elbow dysplasia in the canine population as a whole, says Dr. Greg Keller, chief of veterinary services for the Orthopedic Foundation for Animals, the Columbia, Missouri-based organization that maintains databases and finances research relating to orthopedic and genetic diseases of animals. However, "depending on the breed you're talking about, it's more of a problem in some breeds than even hip dysplasia. The one that comes to mind is the Chow Chow. They list out at No. 1 in affected dogs for elbow dysplasia."

Although the disorder may be diagnosed in one elbow, there's a good chance it's also present bilaterally—that is, in the other foreleg as well. Information from the International Elbow Working Group, a small cadre of canine elbow experts from the United States and Europe who study elbow information and develop screening protocols, found that in a three-year screening of 520 German Shepherds in France, about 20 percent of the dogs had elbow dysplasia and half of that group had it bilaterally.

In a functioning elbow, the radius bears most of the weight, while the ulna acts as a lever for the muscles of the elbow joint. It's the ulna that often pays the price, however, when the joint goes awry. That bone has two features that, in a dysfunctional elbow, can be affected: the coronoid process and the anconeal process, which are bony prominences that bracket the trochlear notch, a shallow curve that cups the end (condyles) of the humerus in the joint.

When correct elbow growth doesn't occur, one of three pathologies that characterize elbow dysplasia may occur. First, the anconeal process may fail to fuse to the ulna as it develops and thus becomes free-floating, resulting in a condition known as ununited anconeal process, or UAP. Second, the medical coronoid process of the ulna may be fragmented, which means that small particles of the bone break free or that fissures form in the structure. Third, the end of the humerus can become affected with osteochondritis dissecans (OCD). This condition results in damaged cartilage and abnormal cartilage formation, which can lead to cartilage flaps that detach and float in the joint. In all three cases, varying degrees of pain, stiffness, and lameness in the forelegs can result.

Depending on the degree of affliction, an owner can manage the dog with weight management, rest, and anti-inflammatory medication. Lameness may occur after hard exercise. Jumping must be curtailed.

Surgical options include arthroscopy, which allows the surgeon to remove floating bits of bone or cartilage through a tiny hole, and ulnar osteotomy, in which the ulna is cut in hopes that by relieving stress in the elbow, the anconeal process may be able to unite to the ulna in a normal fashion.

Other surgical options, including corrective humeral osteotomy (cutting and shaping the humerus in an effort to balance out the elbow joint) and elbow replacement, are on the horizon.

Explore Your Options

If your dog is limping; has problems getting into vehicles or navigating stairs; or does the bunny hop, consult your veterinarian. If the diagnosis is dysplasia, don't despair. Existing and developing surgical options may provide the relief your dog needs. And remember, many dogs' dysplasia can be managed with diet and exercise. ■

15

Treating Arthritis

*Effective treatment can lead to
an active, comfortable life.
The key is early diagnosis.*

Although often thought of as a disease of elderly canines, arthritis (painful joint inflammation) affects many dogs in their prime. While there's no cure for this condition, veterinarians can offer a wide range of treatment options to help arthritic animals live a relatively active, comfortable life. But the key to effective medical treatment is early diagnosis. And observant owners are in the best position to notice the first subtle signs of this debilitating disease.

Arthritis Alert

If your dog begins to take longer than usual to get up after a nap or if your pet who once enthusiastically vaulted into the car now hesitates before carefully climbing in, you should suspect arthritis. Make an appointment with your veterinarian. If debilitating signs appear suddenly, however, your dog may have ruptured an intervertebral disc and should receive immediate medical attention.

Note the arthritic signs you've observed, the conditions under which they occur (before or after exercise, for example), and the approximate time you first noticed the signs. Since most cases of canine arthritis are degenerative (osteoarthritis), usually arising from joint imperfections, make a note of any developmental joint defects (such as hip dysplasia) or traumatic accidents your dog has had. Occasionally, another type of arthritis (inflammatory arthritis) occurs, arising from a systemic ailment such as rheumatoid arthritis or Lyme disease, so it's also important to note whether your dog has shown any signs of general illness such as appetite loss.

Pinpointing Pain

Once you've discussed your observations with your veterinarian, he or she will give your dog a general physical examination and an orthopedic examination. In the orthopedic exam, the veterinarian looks for swelling, heat, or asymmetry between the animal's limbs. He or she will flex and extend each joint to check for decreased range of motion, pain, or abnormal joint sounds.

"Once we've narrowed it down, we usually recommend X-rays," says Dr. Gail Mason, a private practitioner in Brunswick, Maine. The veterinarian carefully examines the X-rays, looking for any changes in the bones of the affected joint. "Joint distension [mild dislocation] and osteophyte formation [bony outgrowth] are typical early signs of degenerative joint disease," explains Dr. Amy Tidwell, associate professor at Tufts University School of Veterinary Medicine.

However, in some cases of early-stage arthritis, the bones of the joint may not yet show changes. Since the composition of the syn-

Hip dysplasia (a loose hipbone-thighbone connection) allows excessive movement between the femoral head and acetabulum. This leads to osteophyte formation and bone degeneration and is one of the most common causes of canine arthritis. If the cruciate ligament (shown intact) ruptures, it creates instability in the knee joint—allowing the tibia to move forward in relation to the femur—which can lead to arthritis.

ovial fluid that lubricates the joint changes early in the disease process, your veterinarian may also drain off and analyze fluid from a suspicious joint (referred to as a joint tap).

Next Steps

Although there is no cure for arthritis, numerous treatments are available to make your canine companion more comfortable—and possibly slow the progress of the disease. You and your veterinarian must thoroughly discuss the treatment options so you can get the treatment that's best for your dog. "Ask your veterinarian to explain the reasons why he or she is recommending a particular treatment and the philosophy behind it," says Dr. Randy Boudrieau, a professor of surgery at Tufts. "If you've got second thoughts, seek a second opinion."

Medical Management

Veterinarians typically advise a three-pronged approach to the medical management of arthritis—exercise moderation, weight control, and anti-inflammatory medication. "The most important aspect is exercise moderation," says Dr. Boudrieau. Too little exercise will cause an arthritic animal to become stiff and sore. But too much exercise may cause your pet to limp in pain. Since dogs can't connect their arthritic pain with an earlier bout of rambunctious play, it's up to you to find a happy medium between exercise restriction and overexertion.

Weight control is also an important part of making an arthritic dog more comfortable. "Some arthritic animals are way too heavy," says Dr. Mason. Excess weight places unnecessary stress on the joints, accelerating joint degeneration. If your dog is overweight, ask your veterinarian to advise you on a weight-loss program.

Exercise moderation and weight control keep most arthritic dogs comfortable most of the time. But your veterinarian may prescribe anti-inflammatory medication for your dog's bad days. Don't give your dog medication without first talking to your veterinarian because "a lot of over-the-counter medications have a very narrow margin of safety in dogs and can cause gastrointestinal upset, such as vomiting and diarrhea, as well as gastrointestinal ulceration," says Dr. Boudrieau. Veterinarians often prescribe a dosage of buffered aspirin, but even this medication has gastrointestinal side effects.

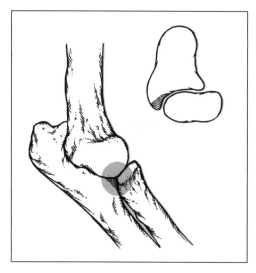

Elbows: In fragmented coronoid process, a small piece of the coronoid process (shown intact) breaks off and "floats" in the elbow joint (the junction of the humerus, ulna, and radius), causing inflammation and arthritis.

Vitamin C

The notion that vitamin C can be used as a treatment for arthritic hips has recently received notice in various media outlets. According to Dr. Boudrieau, there is no scientific evidence that vitamin C can prevent or cure canine hip dysplasia. "Vitamin C is generally thought to have absolutely no effect," he says. "It is not a necessary nutrient for dogs as they can produce their own necessary levels of this vitamin—unlike people."

Rimadyl and other NSAIDs

Carprofen, marketed as Rimadyl by Pfizer Animal Health, is a non-steroidal antiinflammatory drug (NSAID), similar to aspirin. However, unlike aspirin, it is a new class of NSAIDs called COX2 inhibitors. these drugs are formulated to provide pain relief without the gastrointestinal and other side effects sometimes associated with older drugs such as aspirin. Rimadyl has few gastrointestinal side effects, and can be very effective at relieving pain and inflammation. However, since its introduction in early 1997, adverse reactions not seen during various clinical trials—especially acute liver disease—have been reported. Reported reactions also include digestive and renal problems—reactions that are possible with any non-steroidal anti-inflammatory drugs.

While many of the reported adverse reactions involved mild gastrointestinal problems, acute hepatic (liver-related) syndrome was the most severe reaction observed, according to a July 1998 report in *The Pharm Report*, published by the University of Minnesota Col-

❝ LIKE SO MANY OTHER NUTRITIONAL SUPPLEMENTS, THESE SUBSTANCES HAVE ENJOYED A METEORIC RISE TO FAME IN RECENT YEARS. ❞

lege of Veterinary Medicine. Pfizer has modified its advertising to advise consumers that "as with other pain relievers in this class, rare but serious digestive and liver side effects may occur." The company also provides a thorough listing of warnings, contraindications, and potential side effects, in the manner of advertisements for human drugs.

In addition to Rimadyl, there are other new COX2 NSAIDs, such as Etogesic, that may be appropriate for your dog. Very often, the most effective NSAID varies from dog to dog. You should work closely with your veterinarian to determine the NSAID that is best for your dog.

GAGs

A fairly new type of supplement is showing great promise for relieving—and, in some cases, reversing—the arthritic process. The supplements are known collectively as glycosaminoglycans, GAGs for short. The best-known GAGs are chondroitin sulfate and glucosamine.

Like so many other nutritional supplements, these substances have enjoyed a meteoric rise to fame in recent years. The market is now rife with a confusing array of products containing the substances in any number of formulations and concentrations, some helpful, and some quite doubtful.

Rather than simply dulling the pain that results from the arthritis, or reducing the fluid buildup (inflammation) that follows joint trauma, GAGs are chemical reproductions of substances found in the body. These substances are not yet fully understood, but because they are present in cartilage, researchers speculated that supplemental doses of the substances might help slow or stop destruction of cartilage caused by arthritis.

The substances do seem to help the body repair cartilage damage and lessen pain from osteoarthritis, though scientists are still unclear on the exact chemical mechanism responsible for the benefits. Glucosamine is thought to stimulate the formation of new cartilage and help repair damaged cartilage. Chondroitin seems to draw beneficial fluid into cartilage, restoring lost resistance and elasticity, and slowing cartilage breakdown by protecting it from destructive enzymes.

The substances are most often extracted from animal sources; glucosamine usually comes from crab, lobster, or shrimp shells, and chondroitin is most often made from cartilage (usually cattle tracheas, but sometimes shark cartilage is used).

Surgical Options

If medical treatments fail to sufficiently relieve arthritis pain, a veterinary surgeon may be able to give your pet some relief. For example, if bone or cartilage fragments are in the joint ("joint mice"), the surgeon can remove them to decrease inflammation. But since the fragments have often already caused cartilage and bone damage, the joint will likely continue to deteriorate—but possibly at a slower rate.

In some cases, the veterinary surgeon can relieve arthritic pain by eliminating the achy joint. For instance, when hip-joint arthritis is causing pain, the surgeon can perform a femoral head and neck ostectomy to remove the head and the neck connecting the head to the main part of the thighbone. *(For more on this option, see Chapter 14 in this book.)* Small dogs and heavily muscled large dogs are the best candidates for this surgery since they can better support their weight without a joint than lightly muscled large dogs. Alternatively, the surgeon may be able to replace the hip joint with an artificial joint. And in cases of lower-limb arthritis, the surgeon can sometimes fuse the joint (arthrodesis).

Although scientists have not yet found a cure, if you can detect arthritis early, you can help your dog cope comfortably with the disease. ■

16

Aching Backs

Recent breakthroughs offer hope for dogs suffering from debilitating intervertebral disk disease.

Backaches are the bane of many people's lives. But we're in good company—dogs are not immune to back pain either. One of the most painful and potentially debilitating causes of canine back pain is intervertebral disk disease (IDD), the most common canine neurologic syndrome. In addition to back pain, rupture of diseased intervertebral discs can damage the spinal cord, causing varying degrees of paralysis. But due to advances in veterinary medicine, coupled with increased owner awareness, the majority of dogs with IDD recover at least some normal functions.

"If a dog retains the ability to feel pain, it's likely to walk again," says Dr. John Berg, veterinary surgeon and chair of the Department of Clinical Sciences at Tufts University School of Veterinary Medicine. "If dogs have lost (the ability to feel) deep pain for thirty-six hours or less before surgery, 50 percent will walk again and 50 percent won't."

Shock Absorbers

To understand IDD, it helps to envision the canine vertebral column—a hollow tunnel made up of linked, bony segments (vertebrae) that enclose and protect the delicate, gelatinous spinal cord. The spinal cord is the all-important conduit for nerve impulses between all parts of the dog's body and the brain.

Most of the bony segments of the vertebral column are separated by elastic cushions (intervertebral disks) that absorb compressive forces and allow the dog to move comfortably. Dr. Karl Kraus, associate professor of surgery at Tufts University School of Veterinary Medicine, likens a healthy disk to a "jelly doughnut with a rather fibrous outer covering—the annulus fibrosus—and a springy jelly center that absorbs impact—the nucleus pulposus."

Ruptures tend to occur where the spine moves the most, the lower back and the neck. About 80 percent occur in the lower back, the thoracolumbar spine. Others are in the neck spine, called the cervical spine.

Although herniations in the cervical area usually cause only pain, paralysis of the hind legs or all four legs can result if there is significant spinal cord compression. Thoracolumbar disk problems affect only the hind legs and can interfere with bladder control.

"Thoracolumbar is more common by about three to one," Dr. Berg says.

Good Dogs, Good Owners, Bad Disks

Seeing their dogs in obvious distress, some owners blame themselves for having allowed their pets to jump up on furniture or in-

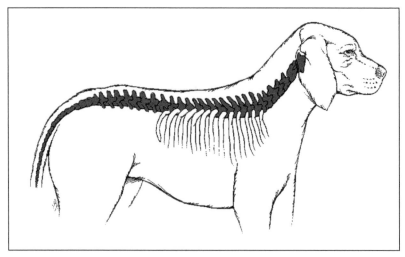

The average dog has seven cervical vertebrae in the neck, thirteen thoracic vertebrae in the midback, seven lumbar vertebrae in the lower back, three fused sacral vertebrae in the pelvis, and a variable number of coccygeal vertebrae in the tail. Only the cervical, thoracic, and lumbar vertebrae have intervertebral disks, making these regions susceptible to intervertebral disk disease (IDD).

dulge in a weekend Frisbee game. But owners should rest assured that IDD does not directly result from just one such event. Full-blown IDD stems from disk degeneration that occurs invisibly and progressively over time.

When a dog has IDD, the disk material undergoes chemical changes, loses its elasticity, and ultimately herniates (protrudes abnormally). The protruding disk material catches the spinal cord between the vertebrae and the ruptured or bulging disk.

In dogs, IDD most often affects the lower thoracic or upper lumbar areas, but it can also occur in the cervical area. IDD occurs less frequently in the upper thoracic area, where rib ligaments cross over the vertebrae and provide extra support.

The signs of IDD vary, depending on the location of the affected disk and the extent of damage to the spinal cord and adjacent nerves. Dogs with moderate spinal cord damage in the mid- or lower- back region, where IDD most often occurs, may suffer pain, rear-limb weakness, and loss of muscular coordination. Dogs with severe spinal cord damage may have hind-end paralysis, become insensitive to painful stimuli, and lose bowel and/or bladder control.

Two Types

Veterinarians recognize two classes of IDD; however, owners may find it difficult to distinguish between them because both compress the spinal cord. Approximately 80 percent of IDD is Type I—the acute form of the disease most common in small, three- to six-year-old dogs, particularly Dachshunds, Beagles, Pekingese, Lhasa Apsos, Shih Tzus, Miniature Poodles, and Cocker Spaniels. These breeds, called chondrodystrophic breeds, often develop disk abnormalities during puppyhood, although the signs of IDD usually don't show up until adulthood.

In Type I disease, after years of invisible disk degeneration, the disk material suddenly bursts into the spinal cord area, severely traumatizing the spinal cord. A dog who seems in perfect health at night may be weak—or even paralyzed—the next morning.

Type II IDD is caused by a bulging disk rather than a burst one. But it too stems from slow, progressive disk degeneration, usually beginning later in a dog's life than Type I. Type II IDD is seen most often in large dogs aged five years or older. Before the disk bursts, the dog may not walk as much as usual and when he or she does walk, you may notice an arched back and dragging of toes.

A full herniation can lead to paralysis of the hind legs and loss of deep pain sensation, which is the ability to feel a painful stimulus applied to the limbs or toes. Veterinarians commonly test for deep pain sensation by pinching the lower structures, slowly squeezing a toe and looking for the dog's reaction, such as looking back or crying out.

A dog with cervical disk disease shows pain through tightened neck muscles, inability to lower the head to eat or drink, and crying when the neck is touched.

Recognizing IDD

The sooner a dog with symptoms gets to the veterinarian, the better the chances for successful treatment. Without its blood supply to carry oxygen and nutrients, a severely compressed spinal cord may die. When it dies, it liquefies. Damage is irreversible.

"If dogs lose the ability to sense severe pain, the prognosis is worse," Dr. Berg says. "If they haven't lost deep pain, chances are 90 percent or greater that they will walk again with prompt, surgical intervention.

Because the signs that suggest IDD do not always mean IDD, your veterinarian will carefully examine your dog before arriving at a diagnosis. Taking into account your dog's medical history, age, and breed, your veterinarian will assess the animal's gait, coordination, pain perception, and reflexes. If the dog is paralyzed and insensitive to pain, the veterinarian may use myelography to precisely locate the disk or disks involved—because serious signs such as paralysis indicate the need for surgery.

During a myelogram, the veterinarian anesthetizes the dog and injects a special dye into the space between the membranes that surround the patient's spinal cord. Herniated or severely bulging disks block the dye's progress. In a radiograph (X ray), the affected area appears as a narrowing in the dye column. But because of the spinal cord's fragility, myelography can be risky. That's why veterinarians may forgo this procedure and rely on clinical observations instead when the IDD seems less severe. Veterinarians occasionally use magnetic resonance imaging (MRI) rather than myelography if MRI equipment is available. MRI results are just as useful as myelogram results, and MRI is far less invasive.

The veterinarian may also analyze a sample of spinal fluid to rule out diseases like meningitis (inflammation of the membranes covering the spinal cord, usually caused by viral infection or immune-mediated conditions) and to test for proteins indicating a spinal tumor.

❝ YOUR VETERINARIAN MAY RECOMMEND

ABSOLUTE CAGE REST FOR TWO TO THREE

WEEKS. THAT MEANS CARRYING YOUR DOG

OUTSIDE TO RELIEVE HIMSELF OR HERSELF. ❞

Rest or Surgery?

The prognosis for each case of IDD is different. In general, the more severe the initial signs, the poorer the prognosis. Chances for recovery are usually greater when veterinary intervention is immediate. A delay of even a day or two after the first signs of IDD appear can mean the difference between full recovery and permanent disability. "In general, paralyzed dogs either recover completely or not at all," Dr. Berg says.

If this is your dog's first episode of IDD-related back pain and a mild loss of motor skills, your veterinarian may recommend absolute cage rest for two to three weeks. (That means carrying your dog outside to relieve himself or herself.) Your veterinarian may also prescribe corticosteroid medication to reduce inflammation. If the animal's condition improves, he or she can gradually return to regular activity that doesn't involve vertebrae-stressing motions like jumping or twisting.

If the clinical signs point to severe spinal cord compression, veterinarians often recommend surgery to remove the invading disk material. Using the myelogram or MRI as a road map, the surgeon will remove part of the bony vertebra in the affected area and gently tease out the disk material—a procedure that Dr. Kraus compares to "extracting a piece of spaghetti encased in a rock."

While some research estimates that IDD recurs in only 5 percent of cases treated, dogs who have a string of degenerative disks and have had more than one episode of back pain are at increased risk of IDD recurrence, according to Dr. Kraus. To prevent a series of ruptures (and surgeries), many surgeons recommend preventive removal of the nucleus pulposus from ten of the most vulnerable disks in the thoracic and lumbar regions (disk fenestration).

Who's at Risk for IDD?

More than eighty dog breeds can develop the disease, also called degenerative disk disease. It strikes both genders, usually those more than three years old, though disk degeneration can start in a dog's first year of life. Certain breeds, called chondrodystrophoid—"chondrodystrophy" means faulty development of cartilage—seem especially affected. In these breeds, skeletal changes that are part of ordinary maturation predispose the spinal disks to change abnormally at an early age.

Some chondrodystrophic breeds have disproportionately short legs, such as Dachshunds, Pekingese, Basset Hounds and Lhasa Apsos. Others, such as Beagles and Miniature Poodles, have chondrodystrophoid disks but don't look chondrodystrophoid. Of all breeds, Dachshunds, followed by Pekingese, are most likely to suffer disk disease.

Disk disease also affects non-chondrodsytrophoid breeds—those with legs in proportion to their size—such as German Shepherds and Labrador Retrievers.

New Techniques

Researchers at the Purdue University Center for Paralysis Research, part of Purdue's School of Veterinary Medicine, have tested several methods of repairing damaged spinal cords. They conducted the studies with the possibility of eventual use on humans. Most recently, Purdue researchers tested polyethylene glycol, or PEG, on paralyzed dogs. A single dose, injected into the damaged area within 48 hours of injury, forms a seal across breaks in nerve fiber. It restores transmission of nerve impulses within minutes to hours.

Two other Purdue trials involved inducing spinal nerve fiber regeneration by applying a weak electrical field to the affected area. Researchers implanted a device producing an electrical current near the spinal column with wires leading to the injured area. In both trials, dogs improved if treated within twelve days of injury.

Purdue researchers also found the drug 4-aminopyridine helped conduct nerve impulses over fibers that have lost their fatty insu-

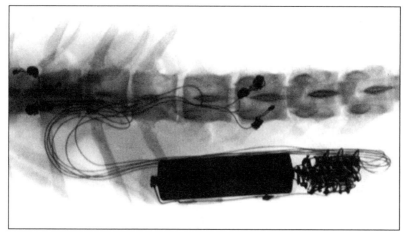

This X ray shows an implanted medical device that produces a weak electrical current to the spinal cord of a paraplegic dog brought to the Purdue Small Animal Hospital. Researchers found the technique promotes recovery if done within twelve days of injury.

lation, called the myelin sheath. The drug, delivered by an implanted pump, helped dogs who had suffered paralysis from disk damage for some time.

Nursing Care

Whether or not surgery is involved, your pet still may need to spend a week at the animal hospital getting total rest and close monitoring. Beyond that, a dog's prospects for recovery depend largely on how well the owner follows the veterinarian's instructions and on the dog's overall condition. Not surprisingly, dogs at or close to their optimum weight have an easier time recuperating.

If your dog is severely disabled, you may have to apply pressure to the animal's abdomen four or five times a day for several days to express urine from the bladder. Otherwise, urine retention could lead to an infection that could spread from the bladder to the kidneys, with potentially fatal results.

If your dog has temporarily lost bowel control, the animal will inevitably soil his or her bed or crate. But you must maintain cleanliness in your dog's quarters to prevent skin scalding and infections. If your dog can't move, you'll also have to change the animal's position periodically to prevent pressure sores. Be sure that the dog's bed is well padded for comfort.

Remember your dog's personal care as well. Use dry shampoo to freshen the haircoat, and continue brushing and combing as usual to keep the dog comfortable. Trim long hair on the dog's buttocks to keep the area clean, and wash the dog if needed after defecation.

Owners should also gently massage and manipulate their dog's limbs to help maintain circulation and muscle tone. Veterinarians sometimes recommend hydrotherapy—placing the dog in a whirlpool bath to stimulate circulation and keep the dog clean. "Towel walking" (supporting some of the dog's weight with a towel slung under the abdomen as the dog walks) is also therapeutic. If your dog seems to have forgotten how to walk, you may have to place the animal on his or her back and gently "bicycle" the limbs to reteach the walking motion.

In addition to giving physical aid, an owner should offer emotional support to a dog recovering from IDD. Some dogs become depressed during recovery and need encouragement from their owners.

Some dogs never regain the use of their hind limbs. But custom-fitted carts are available to support a dog's hindquarters and provide mobility. (Placing a dog in a cart, however, is not a substitute for physical therapy.)

While owners may wish to consider chiropractic or acupuncture treatments to relieve pain, don't eliminate other care in favor of these options. Says Dr. Berg: "For something as serious as this, holistic treatment shouldn't be a substitute for conventional treatment." ■

Section IV

Prevention, Treatment & First Aid

17

What Your Vet
Wants to Know

*It might surprise you to know that preparing for
a visit to the veterinarian isn't that different from
preparing for a visit to your doctor.*

You and your veterinarian share a common goal—to see that your dog receives the best possible care and returns to good health. And while your veterinarian is a trained professional who will carefully examine your dog, he or she needs your help as the pet owner. After all, who knows your pet and his or her behavior better than you?

Dr. John Berg, veterinary surgeon and chair of the Department of Clinical Sciences at Tufts University School of Veterinary Medicine, knows what he wants from a dog owner: accurate observations about the animal's symptoms, including "how often it happens, whether it's increasing in frequency or decreasing, whether it has responded to therapy in the past. Sometimes owners are a little vague about what the problem is, so the more they can observe—and take notes—the better. They have information we can't get any other way."

On average, dogs visit the veterinarian 2.6 times per year, according to a survey by the American Pet Product Manufacturers Association. But for healthy dogs, an annual visit is adequate, Dr. Berg says. While it's unclear whether dogs retain memories of being poked and prodded at the vet's office, "we try to avoid procedures being unpleasant," Dr. Berg says. "We provide pain relief for any painful procedures, and we try to populate our practices with people who love animals and can provide TLC. Dogs get more comfortable with visits over time rather than less comfortable."

Preparing for the Vet

Your trips to the veterinarian will go more smoothly if your dog has been properly socialized. After all, dogs don't naturally love humans to touch, hold, pat, and probe them. The most common areas of sensitivity are ears, mouth, neck, feet, hindquarters, and tail. If your dog has issues about a particular body part, spend extra time there as you work on desensitization.

For example, if your dog objects to having his or her paws touched, perhaps due to a bad nail-trimming experience, try starting on the shoulder or elbow. Touch the animal just above the spot where he or she begins showing nervousness, then feed your pet a treat. Repeat this exercise until the dog looks happily for the treat when you touch the spot, then move a little lower. Repeat until the dog is comfortable with having you touch the paw. You can modify this exercise for all other sensitive body parts. Remember to go slowly to avoid triggering strong reactions.

The more you can do to desensitize and relax your dog, the easier it will be for your veterinarian to make an accurate assessment of the animal's condition.

Making the Most of Your Visit

These steps can make visits to the veterinarian more productive for you, your vet, and your dog.

■ **Keep your dog under control in the waiting room.** An obedi-

The more you can do to desensitize and relax your dog, the easier it will be for your veterinarian ti make an accurate assessment of the animal's condition.

ANDREW CUNNINGHAM, TUSVM

ence-trained dog knows to sit quietly at your feet, even when a pride of kittens enters.

■ **Take detailed notes to the clinic.** When did you first notice symptoms? Did your dog have a bout of vomiting or diarrhea? A change in eating or behavior that could indicate pain? A change in routine? Has your pet traveled recently or been exposed to other animals? How has the dog responded to treatment previously?

■ **Be cautious about medical information you find on the Internet.** "Being informed is important, but a lot of people come in heavily biased about something they've read on the Internet, preconceived ideas of what the disease is and how it ought to be treated," Dr. Berg says.

■ **Ask questions.** What are possible side effects of the medications? When will your dog recover? Will the illness have any long-term effects? How will your pet's diet or exercise regime be affected?

■ **Ask for a referral for a second opinion if you feel it's warranted.** "Owners shouldn't feel bad about getting a second opinion anytime they're uncomfortable with a diagnosis or have been given a diagnosis that's worrisome," Dr. Berg says. "I think they should tell the vet, but they don't have to. It's all part of good communication, and I would tend to err on the side of openness. Sometimes seeking a second opinion can lead to a different diagnosis. We're not always right."

■ **Follow directions.** "If the veterinarian recommends giving medication three times a day, give it three times a day," Dr. Berg says. "Often we struggle with getting people to comply with treatment recommendations."

■ **Don't overstress if your dog has to be hospitalized.** "Most dogs tolerate being hospitalized really well," Dr. Berg says. "They don't get horribly scared. They tend to deal with it much better than owners."

For Puppy Owners

No matter if the source of your new puppy was a rescue group, a shelter, or a breeder, schedule a veterinary visit within twenty-four hours of bringing him or her home.

An exam may uncover a defect or health problem you need to deal with for the pup's sake or that of other animals at home. If there is such a problem, you want to know immediately because you may be able to return the puppy before you become too attached to him or her.

The veterinary clinic will ask you to bring a sample of the dog's stool to check for intestinal parasites. This also is a good opportunity to schedule your new pet's vaccinations.

It's in the Genes

If the recommendations above sound familiar, it may be because you take the same steps before you visit your family doctor about a problem you or your children are having. That's not just a coincidence; we share 95 percent of our genes with dogs, says Dr. Nicholas Dodman, professor and director of Tufts' Behavior Clinic and the author of *If Only They Could Speak: Stories About Pets and Their People* (W.W. Norton & Co.).

Dr. Dodman was among the first veterinarians in the country to treat aggressive dogs with the human antidepressant Prozac (fluoxetine). Careful drug use, along with behavior modification, can save the lives of dogs with behavior problems, he says.

"If you look at the muscle of the heart of the dog under a microscope, you can't tell the difference between the canine tissue and heart muscle from a human being," Dr. Dodman says. "Ditto regarding the kidneys. Dogs' brains and human brains are pretty similar, too. While a trained eye could tell the difference between a dog brain and a human brain placed side by side on a table, the differences are of proportion rather than absolute ones, he says. Human brains have more corrugations, which signify we're more refined thinkers. But human and dog brains do consist of the same basic components, from the types of neurons and their chemical messengers to the structures themselves. Emotions are handled by similar centers in dogs and humans, and memories are stored in like repositories.

Going from head to toe, dogs and humans have many body parts in common, Dr. Dodman says: Spine. Nervous system. Intestines. Spleen. Thanks to a similar cerebral cortex, Dr. Dodman says, "Dogs think. They learn. They have emotions. The similarities are considerably more than the differences." ■

18

First Aid 101

Whether you're providing emergency care or dealing with a minor scrape, it's important to take actions that will help, not hurt, the dog.

F irst, do no harm," Hippocrates wrote. That's good advice, whether the dog you're trying to assist is your own or an unknown animal who has been in an accident. In this chapter, we'll discuss strategies for helping dogs in an emergency situation until professional help is available as well as home remedies that you may wish to employ in consultation with your veterinarian.

When It's an Emergency

If you're coming to the aid of a dog who has been hit by a vehicle, frequently the most appropriate action simply is to "load and go"— quickly but safely transport the injured animal to the nearest veterinarian. In a case like this, always have someone call the hospital in advance so the staff can prepare for the victim's arrival. Your job is to initiate first aid—stabilizing the injured dog until the animal gets definitive, professional treatment.

If necessary, divert traffic around the accident scene, then approach the dog slowly. Protect yourself; even docile dogs may bite when in pain, so consider muzzling the accident victim. However, do not muzzle short-nosed dogs, dogs who have vomited, or dogs who are having difficulty breathing. In such cases, swaddle the dog's head and neck in a blanket or jacket.

Injury Checklist

Breathing

First, make sure that the dog's airway is clear and that the animal is breathing normally. Remove visible upper airway blockages by sweeping your fingers through the dog's mouth. If the dog's breathing is rapid and shallow, there's probably lower airway damage, which first aid can't address. Get the dog to a veterinarian immediately. If the dog is not breathing at all (bluish gums, no discernible chest movement, and no air leaving the nostrils), begin rescue breathing (see illustration) while an assistant drives the animal to the nearest veterinary clinic.

Bleeding

Attend to bleeding next. If there's no visible bleeding but the dog's gums are pale and the heart rate is higher than 160 beats per minute, the animal is probably bleeding internally. Normal canine heart rates range from 60 to 120 beats per minute, depending on the animal's size, age, and overall condition. To check a dog's heart rate, press your fingers directly against the left side of the chest near the dog's elbow. Alternatively, check the pulse by pressing your fingers against the inner-thigh artery.

Dogs in shock due to blood loss have pale gums and feel cold to the touch. Using a jacket or blanket, keep such animals warm during transport. If there is no heartbeat or pulse at all, initiate chest compressions.

If a dog is not breathing, initiate rescue breathing (See Chapter 19 in this book.) Take turns with a partner to avoid wooziness from hyperventilation. If the animal resumes breathing, stop. If not, continue rescue breathing until you reach the animal hospital.

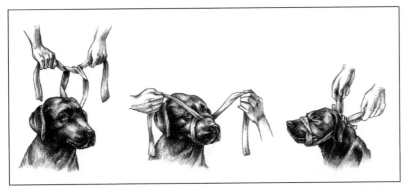

When muzzling a dog in an emergency, use anything that ties, including gauze, rope, nylon stocking, or a necktie. Loop the material and slip the loop over the dog's nose from above and behind the animal's head. Tighten the loop snugly on the dog's snout, but don't impede breathing. Pull the material down each side of the dog's face and tie a bow after crisscrossing the material under the chin and looping it back behind the ears.

Stanch external bleeding by applying direct pressure to the wound. If available, use a compress made of absorbent material (such as gauze, a sock, or a shirt), but pressure from your finger or hand will work. If blood soaks through the absorbent material, add fresh layers rather than removing material so you don't break clots that might have formed.

Head and Spinal Cord

Signs of injury to these areas include unequal pupil size, bleeding from the ears or nose, a wobbly gait, a crooked or humped back, and inability to stand or move limbs.

While these dogs need immediate medical attention, take care that you do not twist the body and make the injury worse. Carefully lift the dog onto a flat, hard surface such as an ironing board or piece of plywood. If such an object is not available, try using a jacket or blanket held taut by several people.

Fractures

Suspect a bone fracture if the dog favors or refuses to use a limb. Fractures are rarely life-threatening, though open fractures (where the broken bone pierces the skin) may be serious. If the bone is not exposed and the patient is amenable, splint the affected limb (see illustration). For open fractures, carefully remove large debris such as leaves or twigs, cover the wound, and get the dog to the hospital.

Secure a rigid splint with tape or cloth strips to immobilize a fractured limb—but only if the joints above and below the fracture can be included. Rolled-up newspapers or magazines, wire coat hangers, sticks, or (for small dogs) tongue depressors are good splint materials.

Home Care

Not all situations, especially ones involving your own dog, are emergencies. Your veterinarian is the one best qualified to determine if you should take remedial steps at home or take your dog to the animal clinic. And even if you treat your dog at home initially, you may need to visit the animal hospital later for a complete diagnostic workup or more targeted treatment. Below, we outline some health problems you may experience with your dog. This information cannot replace the knowledge of your own veterinarian.

Scrapes and Cuts

Dogs often sustain minor scrapes and cuts. Disinfecting such wounds helps prevent infection. In a pinch, rubbing alcohol is an adequate disinfectant, but it stings on contact. Antiseptics such as hydrogen peroxide or chlorhexidine are more effective and less likely to smart. The oxygen-rich bubbling action of hydrogen peroxide is especially useful for disinfecting bite wounds or abscesses, but these types of injuries—and any skin lesion that becomes infected—should always be examined by a veterinarian.

Digestive Disturbances

Dogs are notorious for eating things that offend their digestive systems. If your dog's indiscriminate appetite causes only a touch of diarrhea, your veterinarian may prescribe a weight-based dose of

Pepto-Bismol or Kaopectate to settle the digestive tract. If diarrhea lasts for more than twenty-four hours or is accompanied by vomiting, the dog should be seen by a veterinarian.

If your dog has ingested a dangerous substance, your veterinarian may want to purge the offending material from the dog's digestive tract and may direct you to induce vomiting with the aid of hydrogen peroxide. Never induce vomiting without first talking to your veterinarian; there are substances, such as drain cleaner, that can burn your dog's esophagus on their way out. It's also inadvisable to induce vomiting in a dog who is unable to stand, stuporous, or unconscious. Doing so increases the risk of choking and aspiration; the accidental inhalation of foreign matter, which can lead to dangerous lung complications.

To rid the canine digestive tract of a potentially harmful substance without inducing vomiting, your veterinarian may recommend giving your dog a solution of activated charcoal, which absorbs toxic substances. Activated charcoal that contains a cathartic (an agent that stimulates bowel activity) is best because it is important that the harmful substances be expelled quickly from the dog's system.

Except in dogs suffering hind-end nerve damage, constipation is an uncommon complaint. Consequently, veterinarians rarely ask owners to give their dogs enemas. Enemas sold for people contain high levels of phosphate, which can cause dangerous reductions in a canine's calcium levels.

Chocolate Poisoning

If the chocolate you look forward to savoring ends up inside your dog, you may find yourself making an emergency trip to your veterinary clinic. Chocolate contains theobromine, a substance toxic to dogs. Baking chocolate contains more theobromine per ounce than semisweet chocolate, which, in turn, contains more theobromine than milk chocolate. While most lethal cases of chocolate poisoning occur when small dogs eat large quantities of baking chocolate, owners should nonetheless keep their dogs and chocolates separated.

If you witness your dog eating chocolate or if the animal shows any signs of chocolate toxicity (anxiety, pacing, hyperexcitability, excessive thirst and urination, vomiting, or seizures), call your veterinarian immediately and tell him or her what type of chocolate your dog ate, how much you think was eaten and when, and how much your dog weighs. If you find out about this incident within a couple hours, your veterinarian will either instruct you on how to induce vomiting or ask you to bring your dog to the clinic for stomach pumping. But if more than a couple of hours have passed, the toxin will already be circulating in your dog's system and so your veterinarian will provide supportive therapy (such as intravenous fluids and drugs to control hyperexcitability) while the animal's body is detoxifying itself.

Common Minor Crises

A common at-home "dog crisis" occurs when owners inadvertently clip their dog's nails too close to the quick. A styptic pencil is an effective way to stanch the resulting bleeding. Available at most pharmacies, styptic pencils contain astringent material that, when applied to bleeding tissues, constricts the blood vessels and helps form a blood clot. Be aware, however, that styptic pencils often sting when applied. Some dogs begin to associate that unpleasantness with nail clipping in general, and pedicure time becomes a wrestling match. For some owners, it's best to let a veterinarian or professional groomer clip the nails.

Baking soda is probably a staple in your kitchen and can be handy in dog care as well. Mixed with water to form a paste, baking soda helps take the itch and pain out of some insect stings, and it can be used to help neutralize acid burns.

If your dog has flea-bite dermatitis or other moist skin lesions, you may want to keep an over-the-counter astringent such as Domeboro solution on hand. Prior to using such drying agents, carefully remove the hair from the affected area using an electric clipper equipped with a blade that's right for your dog's coat. It's best to consult with your veterinarian about any chronic skin condition because additional treatment may be necessary.

Sometimes, a dog's eyes become irritated by dirt or a speck of plant material. In such cases, you can use contact lens cleaner as an eye flush. If there's significant redness or swelling or if the foreign material remains in the eye after flushing, take your dog to the veterinarian.

Relieving Pain

Although the risk of administering human pain relievers (analgesics) is greater with cats than with dogs, never give medications containing aspirin, acetaminophen, or ibuprofen to a dog without first consulting a veterinarian. Of the common household pain relievers, buffered aspirin is probably the one most often recommended by veterinarians. But you need about 25 milligrams per kilogram (2.2 pounds) of dog weight—a significant amount—to achieve effective pain relief. Administering aspirin a couple of times at that dosage is not likely to cause problems, but veterinarians are hesitant to dose dogs at that level for long periods of time due to the risk of gastrointestinal bleeding and ulceration.

Watch for Signs

Behavior changes are the most common signs that dogs are in pain, the American Animal Hospital Association says. "Our patients don't tell us when they're in pain as human patients do," says Dr. Link Welborn, AAHA president and chairman of its Standards Enhancement Task Force. "There's a gradually greater awareness that pain exists in animals, and yet it's difficult even for us to interpret."

For example, dogs with toothaches may still try to eat. More subtle signs of such a problem include odd odors or behaviors such as dropping food, tilting the head, gulping food, or suddenly refusing hard kibble.

Here are other ways to tell if your dog hurts:
■ *Reluctance to run, jump, or play*

■ *Inability to lie down comfortably*

■ *Limping, difficulty walking*

■ *Agitation, pacing, trembling*

■ *Panting, excessive salivation, or difficulty breathing*

■ *Refusal to eat or drink*

■ *Incessant licking*

■ *Chewing at body parts*

■ *Barking, groaning, or whimpering, especially when touched*

■ *Aggressiveness when approached or touched*

■ *Inability to stand*

■ *Being non-responsive*

Pet-to-Human Disease Transmission

While there are a few illnesses humans can catch from their dogs, the risk of canine-to-human disease transmission is quite small. "People get more diseases from other people than they do from their pets," says Dr. Susan Cotter, professor at Tufts University School of Veterinary Medicine. But by learning about zoonotic diseases (diseases humans can get from animals), you can reduce the risk of acquiring an illness from your dog to practically zero.

Bite Wounds

Bite wound infections are the most common zoonotic disease people get from dogs. Prevent bites by seeking behavioral therapy for an aggressive dog, and teach children not to jump on any dog or pull the ears or tail, no matter how docile the animal appears. To prevent infection, immediately clean and disinfect any bite wound. People who have had their spleens removed are susceptible to a particularly severe bacterial infection and should immediately contact

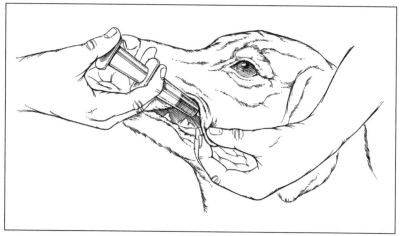

A 20-milliliter plastic syringe will help you administer liquid medication, reducing the chance of splatter and the risk of accidental inhalation (aspiration):

Load the syringe with the amount of liquid prescribed by your veterinarian. Wipe off the tip so the dog doesn't get a preview taste of what's coming. Tilt your dog's head back slightly. With your fingers, form a pouch by pulling out the dog's cheek near the corner of its mouth. Slowly but steadily "inject" the liquid into the pouch. Most dogs swallow reflexively; if your patient does not, gently stroke the animal's throat to encourage swallowing.

their physician if they've been bitten. Dog bites are also a transmission vehicle for rabies, a rare viral neurological disease. To prevent rabies, always keep your dog's rabies vaccination up to date.

Skin Diseases and Parasites

Petting a dog affected with a zoonotic skin disease or external parasites gives these villains an opportunity to make the jump from dog to owner.

For instance, ringworm (a fungal skin infection that causes circular areas of hair loss) and mites (parasites that cause itching and crusting of the skin, particularly on the edges of the ears and nose) can be passed from dogs to humans. If you notice areas of hair loss or skin crusting or your dog is scratching excessively, call your veterinarian. He or she can treat the dog before you start itching, too. Scratching can also be a sign of fleas, another parasite that can bridge the gap from dog to human. Look for fleas on your dog's back, at the base of the tail, and on the abdomen, and treat any infestation immediately.

Contact with the feces or urine of an animal infected with certain zoonotic diseases can give the infectious organisms an avenue for infecting you. For example, if your dog has salmonellosis (a highly contagious bacterial disease affecting the gastrointestinal tract), the animal will shed the organism in the feces. If you inadvertently get fecal matter on your hands, then subsequently touch your mouth or nose, the bacteria can gain entrance to your digestive tract. Internal parasites can gain entry to your body in the same way. (Dogs, however, don't carry pinworm, a parasite that affects children.) Immediately wash your hands after you've cleaned up feces or urine. And make sure that your dog is routinely dewormed and that puppies are dewormed as early as possible.

Owners with young children should be especially alert to their dog's health, since young children—due to their lack of concern about hygiene—are more likely to pick up diseases from the family dog. But the risk of your child picking up a disease from a healthy dog is very small indeed.

Extra Precautions

Cut your dog's risk of picking up a zoonotic disease by taking the following steps:

■ Keep the animal's vaccinations up to date.

■ Feed your dog only commercial dog food and provide fresh tap water to drink.

Minimize the chances of acquiring a zoonotic disease from your dog by doing the following:

■ Wash your hands after you handle your dog, particularly before eating.

■ Take your dog to the veterinarian if the animal develops diarrhea that persists for more than twenty-four hours.

■ Wear plastic gloves and use disinfectant to clean up urine or feces and wash your hands afterward.

■ Wash and disinfect bite or scratch wounds immediately.

Reduce the odds of bringing a dog with zoonotic disease into your home by adopting:

■ a dog older than six months of age (because puppies are more likely to carry disease than older dogs).

■ a dog who doesn't live with a lot of transient dogs who may be carrying disease. ■

19

Canine Heimlich/CPR

A dog can suffer respiratory and/or cardiac arrest just like a human. Here's what to do if your dog requires emergency intervention.

The primary reason that dogs choke is obstruction of the airway by food, a toy, or some other object. Rawhide chewies are particular culprits in that they often break into pieces that can lodge in a dog's throat. Dogs may also choke as a result of trauma to the neck or throat region, due to upper respiratory disease, or on their own vomit.

An anaphylactic (severe allergic) reaction may cause the tongue itself to swell and obstruct the airway. It is a good idea to consult your veterinarian about keeping an over-the-counter antihistamine such as diphenhydramine as part of your first aid kit for the immediate treatment of anaphylactic shock.

Signs of Choking

These behaviors may signal that your dog is choking:
- Arrested breathing
- Struggling or gasping to breathe
- Loud breathing sounds
- Anxiousness
- Bluish or whitish tinge to the gums
- Chasing itself or pawing at its mouth as though trying to remove something.

Don't confuse coughing and choking. While animals in either situation may forcefully exhale, a choking dog will have trouble breathing.

What to Do if Your Dog Is Choking

If you determine that a situation merits intervention, you must perform the following steps to restore your dog's breathing. If you suspect the dog is choking because of anaphylactic shock, you should
call your veterinarian immediately and proceed with rescue breathing. Remember that performing first aid on an animal who is merely coughing can cause injury.

- Capture and restrain the dog.
- Attempt to keep the animal calm.
- Open the mouth, pull the tongue forward to open the airway
and perform a finger sweep from side to side and to the back of the
tongue to see if you can feel and dislodge the obstructing object.
Check in crevices at the far reaches of the mouth, behind the teeth,
and also along the roof. If you encounter a foreign object, be careful not to shove it farther into the throat. Use extreme caution when
performing the finger sweep on a conscious animal. The fear associated with choking may incite the animal to bite you.
- If choking is still present and the dog is small, try suspending
the animal by the hips with the head hanging down. If the dog is
too large to suspend on your own, raise the animal's hind legs and
support him or her like a wheelbarrow so that the head hangs down.
If this positioning does not remove the object, prepare to perform
abdominal compressions—the Heimlich maneuver.

> " USE EXTREME CAUTION WHEN
> PERFORMING THE FINGER SWEEP ON A
> CONSCIOUS ANIMAL. "

The Canine Heimlich

The canine version of the Heimlich maneuver can be performed
whether the animal is standing or lying down. If the animal has col-
lapsed, it will be easier to lie the dog on his or her right side and
perform the maneuver. Lying the animal on the side will also facil-

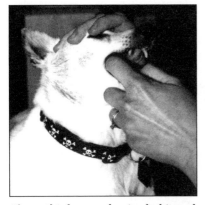

If you think your dog is choking, the first step is to perform a finger sweep, left, which should be done with caution. Open the dog's mouth, pull the tongue forward to open the airway and sweep your finger from side to side and to the back of the tongue. Be careful not to push an obstruction farther down the throat. If this doesn't work, try suspending the dog in the wheelbarrow position, rear up and head hanging down.

itate cardiopulmonary resuscitation (CPR) if it becomes necessary.

Place your arms around the animal's waist and close your hands to make a fist just behind the last rib. If the animal is lying down, brace the back with your right hand and use the left to press against the abdomen. With a small dog, it is not necessary to make a fist; the heel of your palm will be enough of a ball to compress the abdomen quickly and rapidly. Give five rapid compressions in this position. Smaller dogs and puppies require very little pressure to achieve the desired effect. Too much pressure can rupture the dog's liver or spleen.

If the animal still isn't breathing effectively, offer rescue breaths by pulling the tongue forward, cupping both hands around the muzzle and exhaling into the nose. If you are working with a small dog, you can actually seal the lips and nose with your mouth. Again, this should be done with extreme caution if the animal is conscious. Give five breaths. Watch for the rise and fall of the lung cavity and be careful not to blow so forcefully that you overfill the lungs. Even a small amount of air getting past the foreign object will make the abdominal compressions more effective.

If abdominal thrusts in conjunction with rescue breathing have not dislodged the object, try administering a sharp blow with the flat side of your palm between the shoulder blades. Because of the horizontal nature of a dog's body, this maneuver should push the obstruction along the throat toward the mouth. (With a human, a

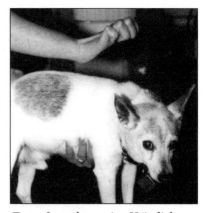

To perform the canine Heimlich technique, steady the dog with one hand and make a fist with the other. Place the fist below the last ribs and gently give five rapid stomach compressions. Rescue breathing can get air to the dog's lungs and also help the Heimlich work. Cup both hands around the snout, and exhale softly five times into the dog's nose. Be careful not to get bitten by a frightened animal.

If the previous steps fail to remove the obstruction, try rapping, again gently, on the dog's back to move the obstruction forward in the throat, towards the mouth. Repeat as necessary. If your dog requires resuscitation, be prepared to administer CPR.

similar blow to the back would serve only to push an object against the front wall of the throat). Again, adjust this blow down for the smaller breeds and puppies. Sweep the mouth once more with your finger to assist in removing the object if it has been dislodged.

If you have succeeded in removing the obstruction and the dog is breathing on his or her own, then you probably have saved the animal's life. If you have not succeeded, repeat the process, beginning with the abdominal thrusts. If the dog has become unconscious, check for a pulse and heartbeat. It may be necessary for you to initiate CPR.

These steps are demonstrated in the Red Cross pet first aid course. They also are described and illustrated in detail in *Pet First Aid*, written by Dr. Bobby Mamato (*see Appendix*).

CPR Could Save Your Dog's Life

Whatever the reason—car accident, electrical shock, near-drowning or other catastrophic event—a dog can suffer respiratory and/or cardiac arrest just like a human. If that time comes, the animal will depend upon a knowledgeable bystander to perform rescue breathing and/or chest compressions. A swift and sure response could mean the difference between life or death.

If your dog is seriously injured or ill and becomes unconscious, breathing and heart action may not cease. However, the dog may go into shock. Signs of shock include shallow breathing, prostration, and diminished reaction to pain and other sensations. The eyes will have a glassy appearance and the gums will be cool and pale. Cover the dog and call or go for help.

At this point, you do need to worry about the body's mechanisms beginning to shut down. Watch for breathing and check your dog's pulse. If your dog's heartbeat and breathing stop, you'll need to perform CPR to save the animal's life. Your dog's tissues and organs require a steady supply of oxygen. If the source is interrupted for only two to four minutes, the damage, especially to the brain, will be irreversible. Signs of cardiac arrest include unconsciousness, cessation of breathing, pale to gray-white gums and dilated pupils.

Performing CPR

CPR consists of two essential operations: rescue breathing and chest compressions. Knowing how to do both and how to do them as part of a single lifesaving effort are vital in a crisis situation.

■ **Be able to locate your dog's pulse before a crisis arises.** You should be able to evaluate your dog's respiration under normal conditions so that you will recognize any major aberrations. The easiest place to detect a pulse is the femoral artery, high on the inner hind leg. Curl your fingers around the front of the leg from the rear and move upward until the back of your hand meets the abdominal wall. Survey the area with your fingers until you find a spot where you can feel the blood rushing through the artery. Count the number of pulses per fifteen seconds and multiply by four. This will give you the number of beats per minute, or your dog's resting pulse.

At the same time, get used to monitoring your dog's heartbeat. Use one hand to monitor the heartbeat in the chest while you monitor the pulse with the other. The pulse and heartbeat should be synchronous. If the pulse is lagging behind the heartbeat, the animal is in danger.

■ **Move the animal from the scene of an accident to a place where you will both be safe while you administer emergency treatment.** Depending upon the nature of the injuries, excessive movement may cause internal bleeding, damage to the soft tissue around a fracture, or additional complications in the spinal column. Try not to jostle the body. Grasp the scruff on the back of the neck and the small of the back and gently slide the pet onto a board or a towel that can be carried between two people like a stretcher.

■ **Be sure that the animal is truly suffering cardiac arrest.** Do not risk performing CPR on an animal who is merely unconscious. You risk having your lifesaving lips chomped on. If you neither see nor hear evidence of the dog's breathing, begin with artificial respiration. If you cannot detect a pulse, you will want to use rescue breathing in conjunction with chest compressions.

■ **Extend the head and neck and pull the tongue forward.** Just as you would with a human being, clear the mouth of any obstructions. As you sweep your finger deep into the throat, you may encounter a hard, smooth bonelike structure, which is actually the Adam's apple, or hyoid apparatus. Do not pull on this apparatus. Sometimes, correct positioning of the head and neck is all that is necessary to initiate spontaneous breathing. If there are no signs of breathing within ten seconds of clearing the airway, proceed with rescue breathing.

■ **Pull the tongue forward, grasp the dog's muzzle and seal the mouth shut by cupping it with your hands.** Place your mouth over the dog's nose and exhale forcefully enough to expand the chest. Once you see the chest expand, remove your mouth and allow the lungs to deflate on their own. Give three to five full breaths and then recheck the breathing and heart function. If the animal is still not breathing, continue to offer rescue breathing, twenty to twenty-five breaths per minute in small dogs and twelve to twenty breaths per minute in medium to large dogs.

■ **Press upon the stomach area every few seconds to help expel the air that may have filled the stomach.** If the stomach swells with air, the rescue breathing will be less effective.

■ **After a few breaths, check for a pulse.** If you cannot detect a pulse, alternate rescue breathing with chest compressions. If your dog or cat is small, you will be able to squeeze the rib cage gently between both hands. Depress the rib cage about sixty to eighty times per minute. Little force is necessary to achieve compression. For larger dogs, it may be easier to turn the animal onto his or her right side with the spine against your body. Place your hands one on top of the other, on the widest part of the chest about one-third of the way up from the sternum. If the dog is on his or her back, place the hands on the breastbone. Press the rib cage or sternum one and a half to four inches, sixty to one-hundred-twenty times per minute.

■ **Practice rescue breathing in conjunction with chest compres-**

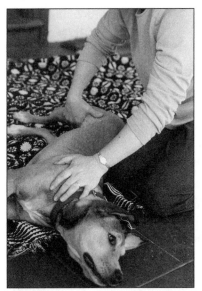

Find the pulse of your dog. The easiest place to feel the pulse is the femoral artery, high on the inner hind leg. Curl your fingers around the front of the leg from the rear and move upward until the back of your hand meets the abdominal wall. If you are certain that the dog has ceased breathing, pull the tongue forward, grasp the dog's muzzle and seal the mouth shut by cupping it with your hands. Place your mouth over the dog's nose and exhale forcefully enough to expand the chest. Once you see the chest expand, remove your mouth and allow the lungs to deflate on their own. Give three to five full breaths and then recheck the breathing and heart function. After a few breaths, check for a pulse. If you cannot detect a pulse, alternate rescue breathing with chest compressions. If your dog is small, you will be able to squeeze the rib cage gently between both hands. Depress the rib cage about sixty to eighty times per minute. Little force is necessary to achieve compression.

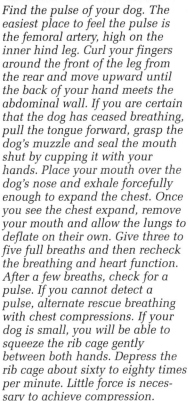

sions on a stuffed animal. (Don't try it on a healthy dog; that could get you a serious bite or harm the dog.) If at all possible, try to give rescue breaths while you are doing the compressions. If this is not possible, offer two breaths after every twelve compressions. If someone is available to assist you with CPR, have that person offer breaths while you offer chest compressions. Coordinate one breath for every second or third compression.

■ **Continue CPR while you make arrangements to transport the animal to a veterinary clinic.** It is possible, though unlikely, to revive an animal after several minutes of CPR. Often, artificial ventilation will be necessary even after the heart has resumed its normal function. There is no determined period of time after which CPR becomes futile. Continue until you can get the animal to a veterinary clinic, or until the pulse and heartbeat have returned to normal, or until you have become exhausted and can no longer continue.

■ **Have your emergency contact numbers posted near your phone so that you can find them easily.** This list of numbers should include your veterinary clinic, the number of the nearest twenty-four-hour emergency care facility, and the numbers for the National Animal Poison Control Center, run by the American Society for the Prevention of Cruelty to Animals, at 1-888-4ANI-HELP.

Most cases requiring CPR are dire. For your dog's sake, it is important to maintain a level of optimism and to use all of your tools at hand. ■

20

Physical Therapy

*In some cases, physical therapy can
help speed your dog's recovery.*

W hether your dog is a couch potato or a finely tuned athlete, you may one day find the animal injured, limping and whimpering or toughing it out in obvious pain. Off you go to the veterinarian in search of relief. Depending on the type of musculoskeletal injury and the patient, treatment may include cage rest, immobilization of the affected limb, medication, and/or surgery. Along with such frontline treatments, veterinarians are also beginning to recognize the effectiveness of physical therapy (PT) in speeding up canine convalescence.

The PT Prescription

Physical therapy involves the use of cold and heat, massage, simple exercises, and several high-tech methods designed to restore normal function, relieve pain, improve muscle tone and circulation, and speed up overall healing time.

But physical therapy comes in many forms, and a technique appropriate for one injury may be detrimental to another. Your veterinarian will help you determine if PT makes sense and, if so, the practitioner will prescribe the most beneficial therapy for your dog. Regardless of the recommended regimen, experts generally advise that you and your dog ease into physical therapy and build up the regimen over a period of time.

Hot or Cold?

Within twenty-four to seventy-two hours after an injury or orthopedic surgery, your veterinarian may recommend applying something cold encased in a cloth to the affected area. Cold compresses
can help reduce swelling and decrease pain when kept in place for
twenty minutes at a time. Cold compresses come in many forms,
from refreezable "chemical ice" packs to a bag of frozen peas straight
from your freezer.

> 66 COLD COMPRESSES COME IN MANY
> FORMS, FROM REFREEZABLE "CHEMICAL
> ICE" PACKS TO A BAG OF FROZEN PEAS
> STRAIGHT FROM YOUR FREEZER. 99

Heat is most helpful twenty-four hours or more after an injury or
to treat chronic flare-ups from earlier injuries. Moderately warm
(not hot) applications of heat will help reduce pain and increase
blood flow, helping to ease muscle spasms and suppress the formation of internal scar tissue (adhesions). Experts urge that heating
pads be avoided because the pads can cause dangerous burns. A
plastic soda bottle filled with warm water and wrapped in a towel
is a much safer alternative for your dog.

After you've warmed up the affected area, your veterinarian may
suggest massage. In addition to mellowing out your dog, massage improves circulation, loosens stiff tendons, and relaxes muscle spasms.

About Massage

Think of canine massage as petting with a purpose. It potentially
benefits a dog's skeletal, muscular, nervous, circulatory, lymphatic,
endocrine, respiratory, digestive, and urinary systems, according to
the American Veterinary Medical Association.

Tufts University School of Veterinary Medicine also recognizes
the benefit of therapeutic touch and now has a physical therapist

Your veterinarian can advise whether physical therapy makes sense for your dog.

on staff. "This is an indicator of the value of purposeful touch, particularly during recovery from orthopedic and neurologic conditions," says Dr. John Berg, veterinary surgeon and chair of Tufts' Department of Clinical Sciences.

"The skin is the biggest sensory organ in the body," says Dr. C. Sue Furman, associate professor in the Department of Anatomy and Neurobiology at the School of Veterinary Medicine at Colorado State University in Fort Collins. She also is the author of *Canine Massage: Balance Your Dog* (Wolfchase) and is the director of the Holistic Touch Therapy Center. "The receptors in the skin react biochemically to being touched. If positive touch is applied on a dog's skin, the receptors signal the brain to release endorphins—feel-good hormones."

Common massage strokes include passive touch (placing both hands on the dog's back while the animal is resting on the ground), effleurage (sliding an open hand over the dog's coat), digital stroking (using the fingertips to move slowly from neck to tail), compression (using rhythmic pumping motion with open palms), petrissage (employing rhythmic strokes to roll, squeeze, wring, and lift soft tissue), percussion (involving rapping, drumming, or patting motions), and stretching (carefully elongating muscle tissues).

"The strokes should never be random but rather specifically orchestrated with a basic plan in mind," Dr. Furman says. "... Always listen to what your dog and his muscles tell you as you proceed, and be ready to adjust your plan to meet your dog's needs."

"Cycling" or "Swimming"?

Keep in mind that your veterinarian may initially prescribe extremely limited physical activity for your dog. Unlike most humans, dogs don't understand how important rest is to rehabilitation. "As soon as they're feeling halfway decent, most dogs want to do too much too soon," observes Dr. Randy Boudrieau, professor and orthopedic surgeon at Tufts. Despite your pet's plaintive entreaties, you may have to enforce strict rest in a warm, well-padded crate.

Once your dog is fit enough to start exercising again, your veterinarian may suggest range-of-motion therapy. There are two types: passive and active. One type of passive exercise is "bicycling" your dog's limbs with the dog resting on his or her back or side. "Passive techniques keep the joints and muscles loose, improving circulation and mobility," says Dr. Boudrieau.

But to strengthen muscles, you need active range-of-motion exercises, where the dog moves his or her own limbs rather than relying on human manipulation. Hydrotherapy (therapeutic exercise in water) is an often recommended range-of-motion technique that allows the buoyant patient to actively "swim" without putting stressful weight on the limbs. You can also do active range-of-motion therapy with a form of controlled leash walking: sling a towel under your dog's body to take some of the weight off the affected limb.

Remember to combine PT with a little "ET"—emotional therapy. A dog who has been through a traumatic physical experience can also use some "pep talks" from the owner, delivered in a loving, encouraging voice.

Don't Try This at Home!

While conscientious owners, guided by their veterinarians, can perform some physical therapy techniques at home, certain methods require specialized equipment and professional training:

- *Acupuncture, performed by certified veterinary acupuncturists, seems to reduce pain.*

- *Ultrasound sends heat from high-energy sound waves into the dog's soft tissues. In people, ultrasound reduces muscle spasms and prevents adhesions.*

- *Neuromuscular stimulation stimulates muscles electrically and may thus diminish muscle wasting, a common aftermath of paralysis from spinal cord injuries.*

And remember, consult with your veterinarian before pursuing any alternative therapy. ■

21

Deworming

Intestinal parasites are tricky, nasty,
elusive creatures. You need prescription
drugs, not over-the-counter remedies,
to eradicate them.

Your dog's body is a smorgasbord for flies, ticks, fleas, mosquitoes, and countless other parasitic invaders, perhaps the most insidious of which rely on your dog's intestinal tract for the completion of their life cycles. Not surprisingly, our contemplation of these often microscopic lives is limited to how best to eradicate them.

"Internal and external parasites are of concern to every dog and cat I see," says Dr. Michael Stone, veterinary internist and clinical assistant professor at Tufts University School of Veterinary Medicine. "I feel it is my responsibility to discuss parasitic infections and their consequences. Many owners are not aware of the dangers that exist for both their pet and themselves."

You'll find a full discussion of ticks and Lyme disease elsewhere in this book. This chapter focuses on worms and other internal parasites.

More than a few of us have been tempted to take a detour to the closest pet store to purchase an over-the-counter remedy against worms. But intestinal parasites span a broad spectrum, not all of which are targeted by the medications found in pet shops or grocery stores. Although it is tempting to equate the swift and thrifty decision with the wise decision, you will never attain the depth of information that a veterinarian provides by reading the package of an over-the-counter medication. An accurate diagnosis of the parasites afflicting your dog is the safest way to ensure

Every State Reports Heartworm Disease

Nearly 250,000 dogs and cats tested positive for heartworm in a 2001 survey of veterinary clinics nationwide, according to the American Heartworm Society and Merial, a maker of Heartguard brand products.

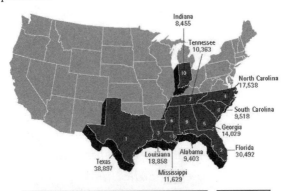

Indiana 8,455
Tennessee 10,363
North Carolina 17,538
South Carolina 9,518
Georgia 14,029
Florida 30,492
Alabama 9,403
Louisiana 18,858
Texas 38,897
Mississippi 11,629

State	Number of Positive Tests in Dogs	Number of Positive Tests in Cats	Percent of State's Clinics Reporting
1. Texas	38,535	362	64 percent
2. Florida	28,749	743	78 percent
3. Louisiana	18,700	158	74 percent
4. North Carolina	17,338	200	79 percent
5. Georgia	13,896	133	64 percent
6. Mississippi	11,522	107	73 percent
7. Tennessee	10,324	39	92 percent
8. South Carolina	9,387	131	79 percent
9. Alabama	9,308	95	83 percent
10. Indiana	8,348	107	73 percent

Healthy heart

Infected heart

The survey involved 25,000 veterinary clinics, of which nearly 18,000 responded; 244,291 cases of heartworm in dogs were reported by the responding clinics.

proper treatment.

In most cases, a veterinarian will conduct a fecal smear or a fecal float to diagnose the parasite. In a fecal smear, a small sample of your dog's stool is deposited directly upon a slide to be viewed under a microscope. Fecal smears are usually done if an insufficient sample of stool has been collected to run a fecal float. Floats allow for a more discriminating view of your dog's intestinal contents. In a fecal float, a sample of stool is mixed with a liquid solution that is heavy enough to float the eggs of any parasite to the surface of a test tube. The eggs can then be skimmed off onto a slide and identified under the microscope.

But treating a dog without the correct diagnosis is a waste of time and, if the true source of the trouble is not targeted, may result in irreparable damage to bodily organs.

Heartworms

"The most damaging of all the parasites is heartworm," says Bert Stromberg, a veterinary pathobiologist and associate dean for research and graduate programs at the University of Minnesota College of Veterinary Medicine. "The parasites live in the heart. They interfere with heart functioning."

Heartworm larvae enter through a mosquito bite, then migrate to the right side of the dog's heart. At maturity at about six months, they can reach a foot long. Untreated, the infection is always fatal.

One study found that about a quarter of a million dogs are infected each year nationally. Hardest hit is the South, with some states reporting infection rates of 50 percent for dogs not on preventive treatments. Cooler areas, such as the Northeast, have a lower incidence as do the arid regions of the West. Despite the availability of preventives—the latest an injectable offering six months' protection—the number of cases of heartworm infection has remained the same for the past decade.

"Heartworm also continues to be a threat because the disease lives on in stray dogs," Dr. Stone says. "When a mosquito bites an infected pet, the mosquito becomes contagious to neighboring pets. Although mosquitoes tend to fly less than a quarter mile, they can travel farther with a strong breeze."

Symptoms include fatigue and cough. As the disease progresses, the dog will experience weight loss, rapid breathing, coughing, and fainting. Blood tests can spot an early infection and give a definitive diagnosis. In more advanced cases, X rays and echocardiograms gauge the severity of the infestation.

Several heartworm preventives are available and are discussed later in this chapter. In areas where heartworm is endemic, owners should give preventives year-round, but even in cooler areas, veterinarians recommend year-round treatment because many heartworm products contain agents that fight other common worms.

Once a dog has heartworms, treatment can be difficult. Different drugs are required to kill the worms at each stage of their life cycle. In the most severe cases, worms must be surgically removed.

It's possible, although extremely rare, for a human to contract canine heartworm. It isn't passed from dog to human, and heartworms don't thrive in humans.

Other Common Parasites

Other common parasites afflicting North American dogs include roundworms, hookworms, tapeworms, and whipworms.

Roundworms

Roundworms (Toxocara canis or Toxocara leonina) are very common. Dogs are infested with roundworms through the ingestion of contaminated feces, through transplacental migration from a pregnant bitch to her prenatal puppies, and through nursing.

"Almost 100 percent of puppies born in the United States are born with roundworm infection," Dr. Stone says. "It can't be avoided. Puppies acquire infections from their mother either in utero or through milk."

After initial exposure, eggs hatch in the intestine. The larvae pierce the intestinal wall and enter the blood stream to migrate throughout the body. Some return to the small intestine where they lay eggs. Others become encysted in the bodily tissues and remain dormant until a stressor, such as pregnancy, reactivates them and they find their way back to the intestines. Still more migrate from the gut into the liver, diaphragm, lungs, and major airways. Occasionally, the worms are coughed up and swallowed, ending up back in the stomach and intestines where they will mature, shed eggs (up to eighty thousand per day!) and repeat the cycle. The worms grow to about three to seven inches long.

Symptoms include abdominal pain, potbellies, listlessness, pale gums, emaciated backbone and back legs, bloating, dull coat, diarrhea, and even fatal cases of small bowel obstruction. Migration of larvae can cause respiratory problems, including pneumonia. Sometimes, owners will spot a full-grown roundworm in a stool, looking like a wriggling piece of spaghetti. Adult dogs will not always show symptoms, though their overall condition may suffer.

Puppies should be wormed for roundworms at four, six, and eight weeks of age, and fecal exams should be conducted at eleven and twelve weeks of age. Treatments are only effective on the adult stage of the worm, so multiple wormings are usually necessary.

"Roundworm infestations are potentially contagious to humans and must be prevented if small children are in the house," Dr. Stone says. Annually there are an estimated ten thousand cases of roundworm infections in humans in the United States, according to the Centers for Disease Control and Prevention (CDC) in Atlanta. Small children are at the greatest risk since they, like dogs, tend to explore

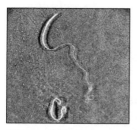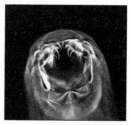

Three of the most common intestinal parasites in dogs are (from left to right) the whipworm, the roundworm and the hookworm.

the world with their mouths.

Once roundworm eggs get inside a human, they can migrate to any part of the body and cause a wide range of symptoms from flu-like aches to blindness.

Hookworms

Hookworms (Ancylostoma caninum and Unicaria) are much smaller than roundworms, and only grow to about an inch in length. They hatch in fecal deposits where they reside as larvae until they are subsequently ingested by other dogs. Like roundworms, hookworm infections are difficult to prevent because the parasite is passed from mother to pup.

Hookworms also can enter the body by penetrating a paw pad, via transplacental migration or through nursing. The hookworm larvae migrate through the body en route to the small intestine. Hookworms, too, may encyst within the muscle tissues during migration. Those reaching the small intestine will mature and commence laying their eggs, up to fifty thousand per day. The eggs are then shed with an animal's feces into the soil, where the cycle is repeated in the next unwary, unprotected dog.

Hookworms feed on blood and tissue by puncturing intestinal lining with oral hooks, resulting in severe blood loss. As few as a hundred worms can result in fatal blood loss in a puppy.

Symptoms include bloody diarrhea, dull dry hair coat, anemia, dehydration and weakness. Dogs will not always exhibit symptoms of infestation. However, in severe cases, intravenous therapy, blood transfusions and extensive supportive care are necessary. In serious cases, multiple dewormings may be required to eliminate the parasites.

If swallowed by humans, hookworms can cause abdominal pain, but a digestive tract infestation is rare. People can contract hookworm by walking barefoot on a beach where a dog has defecated. In humans, hookworms usually manifest themselves in a self-limiting skin irritation that lasts about three weeks.

Whipworms

Whipworm (Trichuris vulpis) eggs can survive in contaminated soil for months under severe weather conditions before being ingested by a canine host. The eggs hatch in the intestines, where they mature into adults. They use their mouths to puncture the intestine and then feed on the dog's blood and tissue fluids. Adults lay eggs in the cecum, which are then shed with feces to repeat the cycle. Whipworms eggs are difficult to attack chemically, so it is important to maintain ongoing treatment and multiple wormings. Dogs confined to small outdoor areas run the greatest risk of infection.

Symptoms include weight loss, pain, watery or bloody stools, dehydration, anemia, straining, and the urge to defecate small volumes frequently. Whipworms pose no threat to human beings.

Tapeworms

Tapeworms (Dipylidium caninum and Taenia pisiformis) are contracted when a dog consumes a flea harboring the tapeworm eggs, or when the animal consumes another intermediate host such as a flea or rabbit or rodent. The larvae mature in the small intestine and begin to shed their eggs with the dog's feces. Often, segments of muscular egg sacs appear in the dog's stool or caught in the hair surrounding the dog's anus. They look like slowly wriggling grains of white rice. These segments desiccate in the environment, where they are then eaten by fleas and repeat the cycle. Mature worms can reach a length of fifty centimeters. They do not occur as often in dogs as they do in cats, because dogs hunt less frequently and have more restricted environments.

"Typically, they don't cause a lot of damage," Dr. Stromberg says, adding that infestations usually have little impact on well-padded modern pets. "If a dog is on the margin of being malnourished, a tapeworm can tip the balance there, but most of the time, with our pets, their diets are more than adequate."

Symptoms include weight loss and loose stools, but they are usually asymptomatic. Most people will first notice a tapeworm infestation by spotting a worm segment squirming on hair near the dog's anus.

Tapeworms are not a major threat, unless they occur in an already immunocompromised pet. Controlling fleas is the best way to prevent tapeworms.

Some species of tapeworms can cause serious illness in humans, but these are rare. "The common tapeworm that dogs get from eating fleas sometimes infects kids who accidentally swallow a flea. The infection is not serious in children, although when Mom finds a tapeworm segment wiggling in the kid's diaper, it does cause some alarm," says Dr. Peter M. Schantz of the CDC's Division of Parasitic Diseases, National Center for Infectious Diseases.

Use Common Sense

The world may be teeming with parasites, but that doesn't mean that they have to live in your dog or children. You can take simple measures to reduce the risk of becoming a host.

- *Make sure puppies or adopted dogs are given deworming drugs on the proper schedule.*

- *Check for parasites and use preventive treatments. "Adult dogs should have periodic fecal examinations for internal parasites and be dewormed periodically," Tufts' Dr. Stone says. "Many heartworm medications contain a dewormer against common internal parasites." Flea and tick preventives also reduce risk.*

- *Keep backyards, streets, and parks clean. Picking up your dog's stool and disposing of it is one of the best ways to prevent parasites. "Be willing to confront people who don't clean up after their pet," the University of Minnesota's Dr. Stromberg says. "You're responsible. Make sure everyone else is."*

- *Wash your hands often with soap and hot water.*

Giardia

Giardia is a protozoan, a single-celled organism that can pop up anywhere in water, especially lakes and ponds, although no open water can be considered entirely safe. The parasite is spread through fecal contamination and while it is often thought of as a disease of hunting dogs, it has been seen in indoor dogs. Dogs lap it up with a drink.

Symptoms can include mild, sporadic diarrhea or violent gastrointestinal upset (explosive diarrhea, cramping, and vomiting), but many infected pets show no signs. Drugs can treat infections and while they can make a dog feel better, they often fail to completely wipe out the parasite. Infected but asymptomatic dogs will continue to shed Giardia into the environment by excreting the hardy cysts in their feces.

Giardiasis, the disease caused by the parasite, is also known as beaver fever, the bane of outdoors types. It's among the most common cause of waterborne diseases in U.S. humans, but Dr. Schantz says most of the strains infecting pets are not highly infective for humans.

The Right Medications

When it comes to the professionals, Interceptor (milbemycin oxime) is generally the medication of choice for the treatment of whipworms, hookworms, and roundworms. Interceptor is primarily marketed as a heartworm preventative, but its effectiveness against whipworms, hookworms, and roundworms gives it broad reach across the spectrum of intestinal parasites. The only common intestinal worm not targeted by Interceptor is the tapeworm, which can be treated with a prescription medication called Droncit.

It is essential that the dog tests negative for heartworms before commencing treatment with Interceptor. Otherwise, treatment can result in a rapid kill of worms, leading to anaphylactic shock. When you consider the absolute necessity of a heartworm preventative, however, it makes sense to treat with Interceptor, which is sold in both six-month and nine-month supplies. The cost of treating with Interceptor varies with the weight of your dog and with the size and traffic of the dispensing clinic.

Sentinel is essentially a combination of Interceptor with Program, an insect-growth regulator used to target and sterilize fleas. If you prefer a kinder, gentler approach to flea control, then Sentinel is an ideal product in the treatment of intestinal worms. Like Interceptor, it is effective against heartworms, whipworms, roundworms, and hookworms as well as fleas. Again, tapeworms require a supplemental treatment of Droncit.

Heartgard Plus is a heartworm preventative effective in controlling roundworms and hookworms, but neither tapeworms nor whipworms. Your veterinarian may recommend Interceptor over Heartgard Plus for the simple fact that it covers whipworms. Again, it is essential to obtain negative test results for heartworm before commencing treatment.

Finally, deserving mention is a medication called Panacur, strictly aimed at eradicating intestinal parasites. It is not a heartworm preventative, but if you are seeking solely to target the gastrointestinal tract, it is the drug of choice. Panacur is effective in the treatment of all four of the most common intestinal parasites.

It cannot be emphasized strongly enough that preventing heartworm through whatever means you and your veterinarian decide upon—injections or pills—must be a priority. Some dogs show no signs of heartworm for up to two years. When they do, they're in the advanced stages, facing costly, sometimes risky treatment and complications and the prospect of a recovery process that can take months.

Beyond Medication

Sanitation is the final word in preventing intestinal worms. It is essential to maintain all areas where a dog spends any length of time in addition to medicating the animal. This means keeping fecal deposits picked up in your yard and providing clean bowls for food and water. Avoid feeding uncooked meat to your dog. If the dog uses a crate or a kennel, or if he or she spends time in an outdoor run, disinfect the entire area on a regular basis, including gravel-bottom pens, with a dilute bleach solution. Sanitation is especially important if you are providing quarters for a mother and her litter. Consider adding a fresh coat of paint to a whelping box to prevent parasitic eggs seeking refuge in the nooks and crannies.

Intestinal parasites exist in all ages and breeds of dogs, but puppies, geriatric dogs and dogs with compromised immune systems are at the greatest risk. Diagnosis is a vital step in preventing future infestations. If you can target the source of the trouble, you can take steps in preventing its recurrence. Do consult a veterinarian if you suspect that your dog is suffering from intestinal parasites, and include stool samples as part of the animal's annual veterinary routine. ■

22

Sterilization

Millions of unwanted dogs are euthanized every year. Spaying and neutering save lives and prevent a number of canine cancers.

M ost people respond with a warm fuzzy "Awwww" reaction when they see a litter of puppies. After all, nothing could possibly be cuter than a bunch of roly-poly baby dogs tumbling and tussling together on the floor. But anyone who works or volunteers at an animal shelter for any length of time soon finds the "Awwww" reaction tempered by the sobering knowledge that millions of unwanted dogs and puppies are euthanized in shelters around this country every year.

For those who regularly deal with the hapless victims of our throwaway society, spay/neuter is a mantra. Rarely, in a shelter worker's opinion, is there a sufficiently valid reason for not surgically rendering a dog incapable of reproducing.

Estimates vary about the size of pet overpopulation in the United States. The Humane Society of the United States (HSUS) estimates shelters euthanize three to four million dogs annually; other estimates put the figure at seven million or more.

More than half of dog owners rank overpopulation as the No. 1 pet issue, yet one-third haven't spayed or neutered their pets, according to a Ralston Purina survey. Among the reasons: the cost, the dog is "too young," haven't bothered to do it yet, plan to breed the dog, "it's not natural," and it's "cruel."

> 66 FOR THOSE WHO REGULARLY DEAL WITH
> THE HAPLESS VICTIMS OF OUR THROWAWAY
> SOCIETY, SPAY/NEUTER IS A MANTRA. 99

Common Arguments

Surgery isn't natural.

There is some truth to this argument. Surgery certainly isn't natural. Nor collars and leashes, prepared dog foods, fences, veterinary care, or the daily killing of healthy "surplus" dogs and puppies. Dogs haven't lived truly natural lives for centuries. If we are picking and choosing which parts of "natural" we want to recreate for our canine companions, we are better off not choosing this one. If we truly wanted to be natural, we would let our female dog get pregnant and have puppies every six months, and no responsible dog owner advocates that.

It's true that every surgery carries risks, but the risks of spay/neuter surgery are minuscule compared to the dangers of overpopulation. Far more dogs die from lack of homes; from mammary tumors and prostate, testicular, and ovarian cancers; and from hormone-related behavior-problems than ever die from spay/neuter surgery.

Sterilization will make my dog fat and lazy.

This concern seems valid. We have all seen spayed and neutered dogs who were, indeed, fat and lazy. But let's think about this for a moment.

Dogs, like humans, get fat if their caloric intake is greater than the calories burned off by exercise and other physical demands. It is true that sterilized dogs often get less exercise. Male dogs who are neutered no longer escape their yards and run for miles in pursuit of females in season or nervously pace the fence in sexual frustration trying to find a way to escape.

Spayed females no longer experience the immense drain on their systems caused by growing puppies in their bodies for sixty-three days and feeding them for another six to eight weeks. Nor do their bodies go through the stress of reproductive-related hormonal changes that result in an expenditure of nervous energy. It's true that sterilized dogs of both sexes are calmer and more content to stay home, but that doesn't mean they have to be fat and lazy. It does mean they are better companions.

It's simple: if your dog gains too much weight, cut back on food and increase exercise!

A Simple Weight-Control Program

- *No free feeding.* *Your dog should get meals, not all-day snacks.*

- *Measure the food.* *Use a measuring cup and dole out a specific amount. Eyeballing it isn't accurate enough; we tend toward generous. A measuring cup also gives us an accurate gauge if it's determined your dog needs to lose weight and your veterinarian recommends cutting back on the amount being fed.*

- *Weigh your dog.* *Pick the animal up and stand on the bathroom scales, then weigh yourself alone, and subtract. Weigh the animal once a week so you will notice sooner, rather than later, if he or she starts to put on pounds. Alternatively, ask your veterinarian if you may stop by occasionally for a weigh-in.*

- *Use the feeding instructions printed on the dog food bag as a guide, not gospel.* *Dog food companies seem to lean toward the generous side of meal rations.*

- *If you train with treats, be sure to count those treats as part of your dog's meal ration.* *If the animal is sufficiently food-motivated you can even use kibble as training rewards.*

- *Give your dog plenty of exercise.* *Throw the tennis ball, a stick, or the Frisbee for twenty minutes a day. Take your pet along when you jog. If you are a portly couch potato, your dog will likely be one too.*

I want my dog to stay intact or experience motherhood.

This is anthropomorphism at its finest. It is usually a male human who insists on leaving his dog intact, perhaps in order not to deprive his four-footed friend of the joy of sex, or maybe out of the owner's own embarrassment at having a male dog without a full complement of male equipment. Stop and think, men! If you have ever watched dogs breeding, you'll notice that they don't particularly appear to be having fun. They are simply driven by a powerful, undeniable, biological urge to reproduce. Unneutered male dogs are far more likely to escape their yards, run free, risk getting shot or hit by cars, get picked up by animal control officers, and get in fights with other male dogs.

> " IF WE ARE RESPONSIBLE DOG OWNERS, WE DON'T ALLOW OUR DOGS TO RUN FREE AND SATISFY THOSE MIGHTY BIOLOGICAL URGES. "

If we are responsible dog owners, we don't allow our dogs to run free and satisfy those mighty biological urges. Our choices are to neuter, and reap the benefits of having a calm, contented canine companion who stays home (and who no longer risks prostate or testicular cancer) or to keep our unneutered male strictly, safely, and unhappily confined to lead a life of constant sexual frustration.

Similarly, the female dog benefits from spaying. While many females do seem to enjoy motherhood, at least at first, by the time their babies reach the age of six weeks most are eager to escape their persistently pushy pups. There are far more life-threatening complications from gestation and birthing than there are from spay surgery. The maternal instinct can also trigger behavior problems; a significant number of dogs develop protective maternal aggression during motherhood. For some dogs, this behavior goes away when the puppies are weaned and placed in new homes. Others continue to display aggressive behavior even after the puppies are long gone.

As noted in Chapter 1 of this book, mammary tumors—the canine equivalent of breast cancer—are extremely common among female dogs who haven't been spayed. Spaying a dog before she first comes into season reduces the risk to almost zero.

"The best recommendation is to spay before the second, third, or fourth heat," says Dr. John Berg, veterinary surgeon and chair of the Department of Clinical Sciences at Tufts University School of Veterinary Medicine. "After the fourth heat, the sparing (of risk) effect is no longer present."

I want to breed my purebred.

Certainly, if we are to continue enjoying purebred dogs, someone has to breed them. Why shouldn't that someone be you? Maybe because there is a lot more involved in responsible breeding than just putting two registered dogs of the same breed in the same room together.

For starters, American Kennel Club papers are not an assurance of quality. Papers simply mean that both of your dog's parents were registered. Ostensibly. Every month, the *AKC Gazette* publishes names of breeders who have falsified records or kept such poor records that the organization has revoked their registration privileges. Even if your papers are accurate and your dog's parents were both champions, that doesn't mean your dog is breeding material.

The responsibilities of breeding should not be taken lightly. If done properly, it is an expensive, time-consuming activity. Prospective canine parents must be checked for hip dysplasia, eye problems (progressive retinal atrophy), and genetic health problems specific to your breed.

Dogs intended for breeding should be outstanding representatives of their breed. If you plan to breed, you need to be willing to campaign your dog on the show circuit and have experts in the breed confirm that your Labrador Retriever is one of the best around. Then you will need to do the research to find the "right" male to breed her to, one who complements her strengths and doesn't underscore her weaknesses.

Once you have gone to all the expense and trouble to be a responsible breeder, chances are your friends aren't going to want to pay the prices that you will ask for your well-bred puppies. Labs can have huge litters—as many as twelve or fifteen at a time. Many of these will be pet, not show quality puppies. They will sell for less than the show quality pups, and a responsible breeder will have them spayed and neutered before they are sold to ensure that they are not used for future breeding.

Don't forget to consider the additional vet bills; you want to be sure your female is in optimal health, and that the puppies get veterinary examinations before they are sold. And, a responsible breeder will take back any of his or her puppies at any time during the dogs' lives if the owner can no longer keep them. Not only may you be left with more puppies to place than you had planned, you may also end up with more adult dogs than you intended to own. Chances are excellent that this hobby will cost you a hefty sum of money rather than make you rich.

Finally, consider that every friend or family member who takes a puppy from you could have provided a home for a puppy at an animal shelter or rescue group. Rescue groups exist for virtually every recognized breed, so if your friends have their hearts set on purebred dogs they can contact breed rescue groups or go on the breed request waiting lists that are now maintained by many animal shelters. Regardless of how many homes you have lined up for your pups, you are contributing to the pet overpopulation problem.

Testicular Implants

The newest thing in canine prosthetics (artificial body parts) is Neuticles—testicular implants for neutered male dogs. Unlike functional prosthetic devices such as artificial hips, Neuticles (marketed by CTI Corporation of Buckner, Missouri) are purely cosmetic. Biologically inert, these polypropylene implants can't produce sperm or the male hormone testosterone. A "Neuticled" dog may therefore look intact, but it can't reproduce. Neuticles can't be retrofitted to previously neutered dogs.

More than 700 dog owners have paid an extra thirty dollars or so to have their veterinarians implant Neuticles as part of the neutering procedure—even though dogs don't seem to care either way.

I want my kids to see the miracle of birth.

Your kids can watch videos that document the birth process. If you want to let them experience the joy (and hard work!) of raising a litter of puppies, sign up with your local shelter or rescue group as a volunteer foster home. For many reasons, most shelters cannot feasibly raise litters of puppies in their kennels, and must often euthanize underage pups. Shelters are desperate for foster homes who can give tender-aged baby dogs a chance to grow up and return to the shelter for adoption when they are eight weeks old and able to withstand the rigors of shelter life. You can even solicit your friends to apply to adopt your foster pups once they have returned to the shelter. You get the joy of puppy-raising and the satisfaction of providing a community service without contributing to pet overpopulation.

My town has solved the pet overpopulation problem, so it's OK to breed again.

"No-Kill" is a myth; it actually means "Someone Kills Them Somewhere Else." In San Francisco, often touted as the first "no-kill" city, more than four thousand animals classified as "unadoptable" are euthanized every year at San Francisco Animal Care & Control, one short block away from the "no-kill" San Francisco SPCA.

In some jurisdictions, an upper respiratory infection (the canine equivalent of the common cold) or a broken leg, both treatable, qualify a dog as unadoptable. Even if San Francisco's four thousand animals were truly not redeemable, surrounding communities in the Bay Area continue to euthanize unwanted animals by the tens of thousands.

> " No-Kill" is a myth. It actually means "Someone Kills Them Somewhere Else." Don't kid yourself; we are far from solving the pet overpopulation problem. "

My veterinarian says spay/neuter surgery is too risky for my aging dog.

This is truly a valid excuse. At some point in a dog's life, the benefits of spay/neuter are outweighed by the risks of surgery. There is no magic age when this happens; it depends on the individual dog. Follow your veterinarian's recommendation if he or she tells you that sterilization is not indicated due to your dog's age and/or condition.

Non-Surgical Neutering

Owners now have a choice of sterilization methods for male puppies three to ten months of age: traditional surgery or a new injectable drug. The Food and Drug Administration has approved the first chemical "sterilant," marking a milestone for animal organizations struggling to reduce the number of unwanted pets.

"This is the first non-surgical sterilization technique to come along in a long, long time, and it reflects, I think, people's hope that new ways can be found to reduce pet overpopulation," says Allen Rutberg, clinical assistant professor at Tufts University School of Veterinary Medicine's Center for Animals and Public Policy.

Veterinarians deliver the shot, called Neutersol, directly into each testicle. It doesn't require general anesthesia as surgical removal of the testicles does, though sedation is recommended to keep pups from moving.

A study of 270 dogs found that 98 percent didn't show discomfort during the injections, according to the FDA and Dr. Don Polley, director of veterinary services at Addison Biological Laboratory, which markets Neutersol. The company suggests veterinarians charge the same fee for the injections as for surgical neutering, which varies regionally from fifty to four hundred dollars. Addison advises veterinarians concerned about pain to observe puppies several hours after the injections and use their discretion about whether to prescribe pain medication.

Neutersol's active ingredient—a zinc compound including the amino acid L-arginine—inhibits sperm production and causes the testicles to atrophy. It's considered 99.6 percent effective in achieving permanent sterilization. One study of 224 dogs resulted in only one failure. Six months after the procedure, the dog continued to produce sperm.

Despite Neutersol's debut, some owners might prefer surgical sterilization. Surgery significantly reduces testosterone production while Neutersol may not, the FDA reports. Unlike surgery, Neutersol may not eliminate some behavior problems, such as roaming, marking and aggression, that cause dogs to be surrendered to animal shelters, the FDA says.

"Behavior problems are a huge reason people give up animals," says Dr. Rutberg, who's also a senior research scientist with the Humane Society of the United States (HSUS).

What's more, the FDA says the drug may not protect against diseases associated with male hormones, such as prostatic disease or testicular tumors.

Neutersol won't single-handedly solve pet overpopulation, however, because it's intended only for males. "That certainly raises concerns," Dr. Rutberg says. When it comes to slowing population growth, "controlling female reproduction is probably more important than controlling male reproduction." ■

23

Clinical Trials

If your dog fits the profile, participation in a clinical trial may provide access to new or experimental treatments.

New drugs. New surgeries. New treatments. All across the country, veterinary schools and drug companies each year are conducting scores of clinical trials. And, if your dog has the disease or disorder being researched, he or she just might be the perfect participant.

"It gives owners access to new, cutting-edge treatments," says Dr. John Berg, veterinary surgeon and chair of the Department of Clinical Sciences at Tufts University School of Veterinary Medicine. He adds that dogs with medical conditions such as brain tumors and advanced organ failure that can't be addressed in a private practice sometimes find treatment via clinical trials.

Some trials, especially those fully funded, offer financial incentive to participants. While outright payments aren't the norm, it's not unusual for the trial to cover all medical costs and veterinary fees associated with the research.

Many of the advances that we make, in oncology in particular, are due to results of clinical trials, Dr. Berg says. "Information we have about the effect of chemotherapy in prolonging the lifespan of dogs with common tumors, like osteosarcoma, very often comes from clinical trials."

How to Find Them

Some veterinary schools post information on their Web sites, and many circulate information among veterinarians in private practice. Owners who take their pets to the veterinary school for treatment are also an obvious source of subjects. It's also possible that using an Internet search engine may turn up a school or drug company researching your dog's ailment.

It can be especially difficult for some schools located outside major urban areas to recruit enough candidates for the requisite research pool. If you live near such a school, that's a point in your and your dog's favor.

Getting the Most from a Trial

Enrollment in a clinical trial might be the only way for your dog to gain access to new or experimental treatments. But getting enrolled is often easier said than done.

The first hurdle is finding a trial. There's no one clearinghouse of trials, so you'll have to do your own legwork. Start with these resources:

■ *Your veterinarian, who might have received alerts or information from institutions conducting studies.*

■ *Veterinary colleges. Most, if not all, will be running a variety of studies and trials.*

■ *The Internet. Start with the search engines such as Google, using the keywords "clinical trial dog." If you find a trial that seems to be a good fit for your dog, contact the person in charge. Researchers often need to be extremely specific about their candidates to guarantee the best results. If your dog doesn't fit the study's specifications, don't fudge. At best, you'll inconvenience the researchers when they discover the truth; at worst, you can skew results and set back important research.*

If your dog is a candidate:

■ *Ask about the pros and cons of the study.*

■ *Find out what's expected of you. Will you need to make weekly visits to the research facility? Give daily medication? Keep a journal on your dog's reaction to the trial?*

■ *Discuss financial considerations, if any.*

■ *Ask about the study's duration.*

Make sure you review an informed consent form that explains exactly how the study is constructed and risks that might apply to your dog.

How They Work

Some research consists of ad-hoc studies that merely keep records of procedures, treatments and results; others are strictly controlled and randomized double-blind studies, meaning that neither the trial's coordinators nor the pets' owners know which, if any, treatment is being received.

For example, if a drug is being tested, all participants may receive an orange pill. However, only some of the pills will actually contain the drug; others would be a placebo, an inactive pill with no treatment value. Trials often compare the results of a drug versus a placebo to assess its effectiveness. The study's coordinators and the participants don't know the pill given to each group, which helps keep the results scientifically valid and unbiased.

This type of study is the gold standard, Dr. Berg says. "However, not all studies adhere to this model, and those that do tend to be expensive. As a result, it's the trials that are underwritten by corporations, research foundations or the government that are often randomized and double-blind."

Studies can take a few weeks to several years. "To accrue a reasonably sized number of patients and then follow them, you're often talking two to four or even six to seven years," Dr. Berg says. "They're not generally three-week deals."

Trials can also encompass more than one location. "Because in any kind of clinical trial, the larger the number of patients, the more believable the information is, often these are multiinstitutional," he says.

Deciding on the number of dogs to recruit can be a science in itself, Dr. Berg says. "To do it correctly, we ask a statistician to tell us. We tell him the amount of difference we'd like to be able to find, if it exists. Then the statistician can in turn tell us how many animals it would take to show that much difference."

For example, if you want to show that a drug can improve an animal's survival by one day—that survival without the drug is, say, 365 days, and with the drug is 366—a staggering number of test subjects would be needed. But if you wanted to establish a 50 percent improvement, fewer animals would be needed to demonstrate the difference.

It's important to remember that studies can also represent a roll of the dice for prospective participants and do not necessarily mean a miracle cure for the dogs involved.

"Sometimes a drug being investigated has side effects, and sometimes the reason for doing the trial is to investigate those side effects," Dr. Berg explains. "And very often we don't know if the drug is effective or not, so there's the risk of forgoing some other known, effective treatment." ■

Appendix

Canine cancer: To learn more, you may wish to visit the Web sites of the Harrington Oncology Program at Tufts University School of Veterinary Medicine (**www.tufts.edu/vet/sah/harrington.html**), the Veterinary Cancer Society (**www.vetcancersociety.org**), the Morris Animal Foundation (**www.morrisanimalfoundation.org**), and the AMC Cancer Research Center (**www.amc.org**).

Canine diabetes: For additional information, see the Society for Comparative Endrocrinology site (**www.compendo.org**) and **www.petdiabetes.org**.

Canine eye problems: More information is available from the American College of Veterinary Ophthalmology (**www.acvo.com/public/op_links.htm**), the Veterinary Ophthalmology Information Center (**www.eyevet.ca**), the Iowa State University College of Veterinary Medicine (**www.vetmed.iastate.edu/services/vth/clinical/ophth/diseases.asp**), and Owners of Blind Dogs (**www.blinddogs.com**).

First Aid: An excellent book for the home is by Roger W. Gfeller, DVM, and Michael W. Thomas, DVM, *First Aid Emergency Care for Dogs and Cats*. Also check with your local Red Cross chapter (courses are scheduled in response to public demand) and with veterinary schools and Red Cross chapters in your area.

Index